50 Wedding Cake Recipes for Home

By: Kelly Johnson

Table of Contents

- Classic Vanilla Wedding Cake
- Chocolate Fudge Wedding Cake
- Lemon Elderflower Wedding Cake
- Red Velvet Wedding Cake
- Almond Amaretto Wedding Cake
- Champagne Wedding Cake
- Hazelnut Praline Wedding Cake
- Raspberry White Chocolate Wedding Cake
- Pistachio Rose Wedding Cake
- Orange Blossom Wedding Cake
- Earl Grey Lavender Wedding Cake
- Coconut Pineapple Wedding Cake
- Marble Wedding Cake
- Carrot Cake with Cream Cheese Frosting
- Mint Chocolate Chip Wedding Cake
- Matcha Green Tea Wedding Cake
- Tiramisu Wedding Cake
- Ginger Spice Wedding Cake
- Caramel Apple Wedding Cake
- Black Forest Wedding Cake
- Cookies and Cream Wedding Cake
- Pina Colada Wedding Cake
- Pumpkin Spice Wedding Cake
- Neapolitan Wedding Cake
- Maple Bacon Wedding Cake
- S'mores Wedding Cake
- Strawberry Champagne Wedding Cake
- Chai Latte Wedding Cake
- Key Lime Wedding Cake
- Honey Lavender Wedding Cake
- Peaches and Cream Wedding Cake
- Baileys Irish Cream Wedding Cake
- Rosewater Pistachio Wedding Cake
- Almond Joy Wedding Cake
- Mocha Hazelnut Wedding Cake

- Blueberry Lemon Wedding Cake
- Earl Grey Lemon Wedding Cake
- Banana Nut Wedding Cake
- Cherry Almond Wedding Cake
- Salted Caramel Wedding Cake
- Passion Fruit Mango Wedding Cake
- Cinnamon Roll Wedding Cake
- Irish Whiskey Chocolate Wedding Cake
- Cardamom Pear Wedding Cake
- Pineapple Upside-Down Wedding Cake
- Raspberry Almond Wedding Cake
- Creme Brulee Wedding Cake
- Coconut Lime Wedding Cake
- Honey Walnut Wedding Cake
- Lavender Honey Wedding Cake

Classic Vanilla Wedding Cake

Ingredients:

For the cake:

- 3 cups all-purpose flour
- 2 cups granulated sugar
- 1 tablespoon baking powder
- 1/2 teaspoon salt
- 1 cup unsalted butter, softened
- 1 cup whole milk
- 1 teaspoon vanilla extract
- 4 large eggs

For the vanilla buttercream:

- 1 1/2 cups unsalted butter, softened
- 4 cups powdered sugar, sifted
- 2 teaspoons vanilla extract
- 2-4 tablespoons heavy cream or milk (as needed)
- Pinch of salt

Instructions:

1. Prepare the cake:
    - Preheat your oven to 350°F (175°C). Grease and flour three 8-inch round cake pans.
    - In a medium bowl, whisk together the flour, baking powder, and salt. Set aside.
    - In a large mixing bowl, beat the butter and sugar together until light and fluffy, about 3-4 minutes.
    - Add the eggs one at a time, beating well after each addition. Stir in the vanilla extract.
    - Gradually add the flour mixture to the butter mixture, alternating with the milk, beginning and ending with the flour mixture. Mix until just combined, being careful not to overmix.
    - Divide the batter evenly among the prepared cake pans. Smooth the tops with a spatula.
    - Bake for 25-30 minutes, or until a toothpick inserted into the center of the cakes comes out clean.
    - Remove from the oven and let the cakes cool in the pans for 10 minutes. Then, transfer them to a wire rack to cool completely before frosting.
2. Make the vanilla buttercream:
    - In a large bowl, beat the softened butter until creamy and smooth.

- Gradually add the powdered sugar, one cup at a time, beating well after each addition.
- Add the vanilla extract, salt, and 2 tablespoons of heavy cream or milk. Beat on medium-high speed for 3-4 minutes until light and fluffy. Add more cream or milk if needed to achieve a spreadable consistency.

3. Assemble the cake:
   - Once the cakes are completely cooled, level the tops if necessary using a serrated knife.
   - Place one cake layer on a serving plate or cake stand. Spread a layer of vanilla buttercream evenly over the top.
   - Repeat with the second cake layer, more buttercream, and then add the third cake layer on top.
   - Frost the entire cake with a thin layer of buttercream to create a crumb coat. Chill the cake in the refrigerator for 30 minutes to set the crumb coat.
   - Finish frosting the cake with the remaining buttercream, smoothing the sides and top with an offset spatula or bench scraper.
4. Decorate (optional):
   - Decorate the cake as desired with fresh flowers, edible pearls, or other decorations suitable for a wedding cake.
5. Serve and enjoy!
   - Let the cake sit at room temperature for about 30 minutes before serving to allow the buttercream to soften slightly.

This classic vanilla wedding cake is sure to be a hit with its tender crumb, rich buttercream, and comforting vanilla flavor—a perfect centerpiece for any wedding celebration!

Chocolate Fudge Wedding Cake

Ingredients:

For the chocolate cake:

- 2 cups granulated sugar
- 1 3/4 cups all-purpose flour
- 3/4 cup unsweetened cocoa powder
- 1 1/2 teaspoons baking powder
- 1 1/2 teaspoons baking soda
- 1 teaspoon salt
- 2 large eggs
- 1 cup whole milk
- 1/2 cup vegetable oil
- 2 teaspoons vanilla extract
- 1 cup boiling water

For the chocolate fudge frosting:

- 1 cup unsalted butter, softened
- 4 cups powdered sugar, sifted
- 3/4 cup unsweetened cocoa powder
- 1/2 cup heavy cream
- 1 teaspoon vanilla extract
- Pinch of salt

Instructions:

1. Prepare the chocolate cake:
    - Preheat your oven to 350°F (175°C). Grease and flour three 8-inch round cake pans.
    - In a large mixing bowl, whisk together the sugar, flour, cocoa powder, baking powder, baking soda, and salt.
    - Add the eggs, milk, oil, and vanilla extract. Beat on medium speed for 2 minutes.
    - Stir in the boiling water. The batter will be thin; this is normal.
    - Divide the batter evenly among the prepared cake pans.
    - Bake for 30-35 minutes, or until a toothpick inserted into the center of the cakes comes out clean.
    - Remove from the oven and let the cakes cool in the pans for 10 minutes. Then, transfer them to a wire rack to cool completely before frosting.
2. Make the chocolate fudge frosting:
    - In a large bowl, beat the softened butter until creamy and smooth.
    - Gradually add the powdered sugar and cocoa powder, alternating with the heavy cream, beating well after each addition.

- Add the vanilla extract and a pinch of salt. Beat on medium-high speed for 3-4 minutes until light and fluffy. Add more cream if needed to achieve a spreadable consistency.
3. Assemble the cake:
     - Once the cakes are completely cooled, level the tops if necessary using a serrated knife.
     - Place one cake layer on a serving plate or cake stand. Spread a layer of chocolate fudge frosting evenly over the top.
     - Repeat with the second cake layer and more frosting, then add the third cake layer on top.
     - Frost the entire cake with a thin layer of frosting to create a crumb coat. Chill the cake in the refrigerator for 30 minutes to set the crumb coat.
     - Finish frosting the cake with the remaining chocolate fudge frosting, smoothing the sides and top with an offset spatula or bench scraper.
4. Decorate (optional):
     - Decorate the cake as desired with chocolate curls, sprinkles, or fresh berries. You can also add a few fresh flowers for a wedding-appropriate touch.
5. Serve and enjoy!
     - Let the cake sit at room temperature for about 30 minutes before serving to allow the frosting to soften slightly.

This chocolate fudge wedding cake is rich, moist, and indulgent—a perfect choice for celebrating a special wedding day with chocolate lovers in mind!

Lemon Elderflower Wedding Cake

Ingredients:

For the lemon elderflower cake:

- 3 cups cake flour
- 1 tablespoon baking powder
- 1/2 teaspoon salt
- 1 cup unsalted butter, softened
- 2 cups granulated sugar
- 4 large eggs
- 1 tablespoon lemon zest (from about 2 lemons)
- 1/4 cup fresh lemon juice
- 1 cup whole milk
- 1 teaspoon vanilla extract
- 1/4 cup elderflower liqueur (such as St-Germain)

For the elderflower syrup:

- 1/2 cup water
- 1/2 cup granulated sugar
- 1/4 cup elderflower liqueur

For the lemon elderflower buttercream:

- 1 1/2 cups unsalted butter, softened
- 5 cups powdered sugar, sifted
- 2 tablespoons fresh lemon juice
- 2 tablespoons elderflower liqueur
- 1 teaspoon lemon zest
- Pinch of salt

Instructions:

1. Prepare the lemon elderflower cake:
    - Preheat your oven to 350°F (175°C). Grease and flour three 8-inch round cake pans.
    - In a medium bowl, sift together the cake flour, baking powder, and salt. Set aside.
    - In a large mixing bowl, cream the butter and sugar together until light and fluffy.
    - Add the eggs one at a time, beating well after each addition.
    - Mix in the lemon zest, lemon juice, and vanilla extract.
    - Gradually add the flour mixture to the butter mixture in three additions, alternating with the milk, beginning and ending with the flour mixture. Mix until just combined.
    - Stir in the elderflower liqueur until evenly incorporated.

- Divide the batter evenly among the prepared cake pans.
- Bake for 25-30 minutes, or until a toothpick inserted into the center of the cakes comes out clean.
- Remove from the oven and let the cakes cool in the pans for 10 minutes. Then, transfer them to a wire rack to cool completely before assembling.

2. Make the elderflower syrup:
    - In a small saucepan, combine the water and sugar over medium heat. Stir until the sugar is dissolved.
    - Remove from heat and stir in the elderflower liqueur. Let the syrup cool completely.

3. Make the lemon elderflower buttercream:
    - In a large bowl, beat the softened butter until creamy and smooth.
    - Gradually add the powdered sugar, one cup at a time, beating well after each addition.
    - Mix in the fresh lemon juice, elderflower liqueur, lemon zest, and a pinch of salt.
    - Beat on medium-high speed for 3-4 minutes until light and fluffy. Add more powdered sugar if needed to adjust the consistency.

4. Assemble the cake:
    - Once the cakes are completely cooled, level the tops if necessary using a serrated knife.
    - Brush each cake layer generously with the elderflower syrup.
    - Place one cake layer on a serving plate or cake stand. Spread a layer of lemon elderflower buttercream evenly over the top.
    - Repeat with the second and third cake layers, spreading buttercream between each layer.
    - Frost the entire cake with a thin layer of buttercream to create a crumb coat. Chill the cake in the refrigerator for 30 minutes to set the crumb coat.
    - Finish frosting the cake with the remaining lemon elderflower buttercream, smoothing the sides and top with an offset spatula or bench scraper.

5. Decorate (optional):
    - Garnish the cake with edible flowers, lemon slices, or elderflower petals for an elegant finish.

6. Serve and enjoy!
    - Let the cake sit at room temperature for about 30 minutes before serving to allow the buttercream to soften slightly.

This Lemon Elderflower Wedding Cake is a delightful blend of citrus and floral flavors, perfect for celebrating a special occasion like a wedding with its refreshing taste and elegant presentation.

Red Velvet Wedding Cake

Ingredients:

For the cake:

- 2 1/2 cups cake flour
- 1 1/2 cups granulated sugar
- 1 teaspoon baking soda
- 1 teaspoon salt
- 2 tablespoons unsweetened cocoa powder
- 1 cup vegetable oil
- 1 cup buttermilk, room temperature
- 2 large eggs, room temperature
- 2 tablespoons red food coloring
- 1 teaspoon vanilla extract
- 1 teaspoon white vinegar

For the cream cheese frosting:

- 16 ounces cream cheese, softened
- 1 cup unsalted butter, softened
- 4 cups powdered sugar, sifted
- 1 teaspoon vanilla extract

Instructions:

1. Prepare the cake:
    - Preheat your oven to 350°F (175°C). Grease and flour three 8-inch round cake pans.
    - In a large bowl, sift together the cake flour, sugar, baking soda, salt, and cocoa powder.
    - In another bowl, whisk together the vegetable oil, buttermilk, eggs, red food coloring, vanilla extract, and white vinegar until well combined.
    - Gradually add the wet ingredients to the dry ingredients, mixing until smooth and well combined.
    - Divide the batter evenly among the prepared cake pans.
    - Bake for 25-30 minutes, or until a toothpick inserted into the center of the cakes comes out clean.
    - Remove from the oven and let the cakes cool in the pans for 10 minutes. Then, transfer them to a wire rack to cool completely before frosting.
2. Make the cream cheese frosting:
    - In a large bowl, beat the softened cream cheese and butter together until smooth and creamy.

- Gradually add the powdered sugar, one cup at a time, beating well after each addition.
- Mix in the vanilla extract until smooth and fluffy. If the frosting is too soft, refrigerate for 30 minutes before using.

3. Assemble the cake:
    - Once the cakes are completely cooled, level the tops if necessary using a serrated knife.
    - Place one cake layer on a serving plate or cake stand. Spread a layer of cream cheese frosting evenly over the top.
    - Repeat with the second and third cake layers, spreading frosting between each layer.
    - Frost the entire cake with a thin layer of frosting to create a crumb coat. Chill the cake in the refrigerator for 30 minutes to set the crumb coat.
    - Finish frosting the cake with the remaining cream cheese frosting, smoothing the sides and top with an offset spatula or bench scraper.
4. Decorate (optional):
    - Decorate the cake as desired with red velvet cake crumbs, fresh berries, or edible rose petals for a beautiful presentation.
5. Serve and enjoy!
    - Let the cake sit at room temperature for about 30 minutes before serving to allow the frosting to soften slightly.

This Red Velvet Wedding Cake is sure to impress with its vibrant color, moist texture, and delicious cream cheese frosting—a perfect centerpiece for celebrating a special wedding day!

Almond Amaretto Wedding Cake

Ingredients:

For the cake:

- 3 cups cake flour
- 1 tablespoon baking powder
- 1/2 teaspoon baking soda
- 1/2 teaspoon salt
- 1 cup unsalted butter, softened
- 2 cups granulated sugar
- 4 large eggs
- 1 cup sour cream
- 1/2 cup whole milk
- 1/4 cup amaretto liqueur
- 1 teaspoon almond extract

For the almond amaretto buttercream:

- 1 1/2 cups unsalted butter, softened
- 5 cups powdered sugar, sifted
- 1/4 cup amaretto liqueur
- 1 teaspoon almond extract
- 1/4 cup heavy cream (or as needed)
- Sliced almonds, toasted (for garnish, optional)

Instructions:

1. Prepare the cake:
    - Preheat your oven to 350°F (175°C). Grease and flour three 8-inch round cake pans.
    - In a medium bowl, sift together the cake flour, baking powder, baking soda, and salt.
    - In a large mixing bowl, cream the softened butter and granulated sugar until light and fluffy.
    - Add the eggs one at a time, mixing well after each addition.
    - Mix in the sour cream, whole milk, amaretto liqueur, and almond extract until smooth and well combined.
    - Gradually add the dry ingredients to the wet ingredients, mixing until just combined.
    - Divide the batter evenly among the prepared cake pans.
    - Bake for 25-30 minutes, or until a toothpick inserted into the center of the cakes comes out clean.

- Remove from the oven and let the cakes cool in the pans for 10 minutes. Then, transfer them to a wire rack to cool completely before frosting.
2. Make the almond amaretto buttercream:
    - In a large bowl, beat the softened butter until creamy and smooth.
    - Gradually add the powdered sugar, one cup at a time, beating well after each addition.
    - Mix in the amaretto liqueur and almond extract.
    - Add the heavy cream, a tablespoon at a time, until the frosting reaches a spreadable consistency.
3. Assemble the cake:
    - Once the cakes are completely cooled, level the tops if necessary using a serrated knife.
    - Place one cake layer on a serving plate or cake stand. Spread a layer of almond amaretto buttercream evenly over the top.
    - Repeat with the second and third cake layers, spreading buttercream between each layer.
    - Frost the entire cake with a thin layer of buttercream to create a crumb coat. Chill the cake in the refrigerator for 30 minutes to set the crumb coat.
    - Finish frosting the cake with the remaining almond amaretto buttercream, smoothing the sides and top with an offset spatula or bench scraper.
4. Decorate (optional):
    - Garnish the cake with toasted sliced almonds around the sides or on top for added crunch and decoration.
5. Serve and enjoy!
    - Let the cake sit at room temperature for about 30 minutes before serving to allow the buttercream to soften slightly.

This Almond Amaretto Wedding Cake is rich with almond flavor and has a delightful hint of amaretto, making it a perfect choice for celebrating a wedding or any special occasion.

Champagne Wedding Cake

Ingredients:

For the cake:

- 3 cups cake flour
- 1 tablespoon baking powder
- 1/2 teaspoon baking soda
- 1/2 teaspoon salt
- 1 cup unsalted butter, softened
- 2 cups granulated sugar
- 4 large eggs
- 1 cup champagne, at room temperature
- 1/2 cup whole milk
- 1 teaspoon vanilla extract

For the champagne buttercream:

- 1 1/2 cups unsalted butter, softened
- 5 cups powdered sugar, sifted
- 1/2 cup champagne, at room temperature
- 1 teaspoon vanilla extract
- Edible gold leaf or sprinkles (for decoration, optional)

Instructions:

1. Prepare the cake:
    - Preheat your oven to 350°F (175°C). Grease and flour three 8-inch round cake pans.
    - In a medium bowl, sift together the cake flour, baking powder, baking soda, and salt.
    - In a large mixing bowl, cream the softened butter and granulated sugar until light and fluffy.
    - Add the eggs one at a time, mixing well after each addition.
    - Mix in the champagne, whole milk, and vanilla extract until smooth and well combined.
    - Gradually add the dry ingredients to the wet ingredients, mixing until just combined.
    - Divide the batter evenly among the prepared cake pans.
    - Bake for 25-30 minutes, or until a toothpick inserted into the center of the cakes comes out clean.
    - Remove from the oven and let the cakes cool in the pans for 10 minutes. Then, transfer them to a wire rack to cool completely before frosting.
2. Make the champagne buttercream:

- In a large bowl, beat the softened butter until creamy and smooth.
- Gradually add the powdered sugar, one cup at a time, beating well after each addition.
- Mix in the champagne and vanilla extract until smooth and fluffy. Adjust the consistency with more powdered sugar if needed.

3. Assemble the cake:
    - Once the cakes are completely cooled, level the tops if necessary using a serrated knife.
    - Place one cake layer on a serving plate or cake stand. Spread a layer of champagne buttercream evenly over the top.
    - Repeat with the second and third cake layers, spreading buttercream between each layer.
    - Frost the entire cake with a thin layer of buttercream to create a crumb coat. Chill the cake in the refrigerator for 30 minutes to set the crumb coat.
    - Finish frosting the cake with the remaining champagne buttercream, smoothing the sides and top with an offset spatula or bench scraper.
4. Decorate (optional):
    - Decorate the cake with edible gold leaf, gold sprinkles, or fresh flowers for an elegant touch befitting a wedding celebration.
5. Serve and enjoy!
    - Let the cake sit at room temperature for about 30 minutes before serving to allow the buttercream to soften slightly.

This Champagne Wedding Cake is light, moist, and infused with the delicate flavor of champagne, making it a perfect centerpiece for a wedding reception. Its elegant appearance and delicious taste are sure to impress guests and make your celebration memorable.

Hazelnut Praline Wedding Cake

Ingredients:

For the hazelnut cake:

- 2 cups cake flour
- 2 teaspoons baking powder
- 1/2 teaspoon baking soda
- 1/2 teaspoon salt
- 1 cup unsalted butter, softened
- 1 1/2 cups granulated sugar
- 4 large eggs
- 1 cup buttermilk
- 1 teaspoon vanilla extract
- 1 cup finely ground hazelnuts

For the hazelnut praline crunch:

- 1 cup granulated sugar
- 1 cup hazelnuts, toasted and roughly chopped

For the hazelnut buttercream:

- 1 1/2 cups unsalted butter, softened
- 5 cups powdered sugar, sifted
- 1/4 cup heavy cream
- 1 teaspoon vanilla extract
- 1/2 cup hazelnut praline paste (store-bought or homemade)

Instructions:

1. Prepare the hazelnut cake:
    - Preheat your oven to 350°F (175°C). Grease and flour three 8-inch round cake pans.
    - In a medium bowl, sift together the cake flour, baking powder, baking soda, and salt.
    - In a large mixing bowl, cream the softened butter and granulated sugar until light and fluffy.
    - Add the eggs one at a time, mixing well after each addition.
    - Mix in the buttermilk and vanilla extract until smooth and well combined.
    - Gradually add the dry ingredients to the wet ingredients, mixing until just combined.
    - Fold in the finely ground hazelnuts until evenly distributed.
    - Divide the batter evenly among the prepared cake pans.

- Bake for 25-30 minutes, or until a toothpick inserted into the center of the cakes comes out clean.
- Remove from the oven and let the cakes cool in the pans for 10 minutes. Then, transfer them to a wire rack to cool completely before frosting.
2. Make the hazelnut praline crunch:
    - Line a baking sheet with parchment paper.
    - In a heavy-bottomed saucepan, heat the granulated sugar over medium heat, stirring constantly with a wooden spoon or heatproof spatula.
    - Once the sugar has melted and turned a deep amber color, stir in the toasted hazelnuts.
    - Quickly pour the mixture onto the prepared baking sheet, spreading it out into an even layer.
    - Let the praline cool completely, then break it into small pieces. Pulse in a food processor until coarsely ground. Set aside.
3. Make the hazelnut buttercream:
    - In a large bowl, beat the softened butter until creamy and smooth.
    - Gradually add the powdered sugar, one cup at a time, beating well after each addition.
    - Mix in the heavy cream and vanilla extract until smooth and fluffy.
    - Add the hazelnut praline paste and beat until well incorporated.
4. Assemble the cake:
    - Once the cakes are completely cooled, level the tops if necessary using a serrated knife.
    - Place one cake layer on a serving plate or cake stand. Spread a layer of hazelnut buttercream evenly over the top.
    - Sprinkle a generous amount of hazelnut praline crunch over the buttercream.
    - Repeat with the second and third cake layers, spreading buttercream and praline crunch between each layer.
    - Frost the entire cake with a thin layer of buttercream to create a crumb coat. Chill the cake in the refrigerator for 30 minutes to set the crumb coat.
    - Finish frosting the cake with the remaining hazelnut buttercream, smoothing the sides and top with an offset spatula or bench scraper.
5. Decorate (optional):
    - Garnish the top of the cake with additional hazelnut praline crunch or whole toasted hazelnuts for decoration.
6. Serve and enjoy!
    - Let the cake sit at room temperature for about 30 minutes before serving to allow the buttercream to soften slightly.

This Hazelnut Praline Wedding Cake is a show-stopping dessert, perfect for celebrating a special wedding day with its rich hazelnut flavor and delightful crunch from the praline. It's sure to impress and delight your guests!

Raspberry White Chocolate Wedding Cake

Ingredients:

For the cake:

- 3 cups cake flour
- 1 tablespoon baking powder
- 1/2 teaspoon baking soda
- 1/2 teaspoon salt
- 1 cup unsalted butter, softened
- 2 cups granulated sugar
- 4 large eggs
- 1 cup buttermilk
- 1 teaspoon vanilla extract
- 4 ounces white chocolate, melted and cooled
- 1 cup fresh raspberries, chopped

For the raspberry filling:

- 2 cups fresh raspberries
- 1/4 cup granulated sugar
- 1 tablespoon cornstarch
- 1 tablespoon lemon juice

For the white chocolate buttercream:

- 1 1/2 cups unsalted butter, softened
- 5 cups powdered sugar, sifted
- 8 ounces white chocolate, melted and cooled
- 1 teaspoon vanilla extract
- 2-4 tablespoons heavy cream (as needed)

Instructions:

1. Prepare the cake:
    - Preheat your oven to 350°F (175°C). Grease and flour three 8-inch round cake pans.
    - In a medium bowl, sift together the cake flour, baking powder, baking soda, and salt.
    - In a large mixing bowl, cream the softened butter and granulated sugar until light and fluffy.
    - Add the eggs one at a time, mixing well after each addition.
    - Mix in the buttermilk and vanilla extract until smooth and well combined.
    - Gradually add the dry ingredients to the wet ingredients, mixing until just combined.

- Fold in the melted white chocolate until evenly distributed.
- Gently fold in the chopped raspberries.
- Divide the batter evenly among the prepared cake pans.
- Bake for 25-30 minutes, or until a toothpick inserted into the center of the cakes comes out clean.
- Remove from the oven and let the cakes cool in the pans for 10 minutes. Then, transfer them to a wire rack to cool completely before assembling.

2. Make the raspberry filling:
    - In a saucepan, combine the fresh raspberries, granulated sugar, cornstarch, and lemon juice.
    - Cook over medium heat, stirring frequently, until the mixture thickens and the raspberries break down, about 5-7 minutes.
    - Remove from heat and strain the mixture through a fine mesh sieve to remove seeds. Let the raspberry filling cool completely.
3. Make the white chocolate buttercream:
    - In a large bowl, beat the softened butter until creamy and smooth.
    - Gradually add the powdered sugar, one cup at a time, beating well after each addition.
    - Mix in the melted and cooled white chocolate until smooth and well combined.
    - Add the vanilla extract and enough heavy cream to achieve a spreadable consistency, beating on medium-high speed for 3-4 minutes until light and fluffy.
4. Assemble the cake:
    - Once the cakes are completely cooled, level the tops if necessary using a serrated knife.
    - Place one cake layer on a serving plate or cake stand. Spread a layer of white chocolate buttercream evenly over the top.
    - Pipe a border of buttercream around the edge to create a dam, then spread a layer of raspberry filling within the dam.
    - Repeat with the second cake layer, more buttercream, and raspberry filling, then add the third cake layer on top.
    - Frost the entire cake with a thin layer of buttercream to create a crumb coat. Chill the cake in the refrigerator for 30 minutes to set the crumb coat.
    - Finish frosting the cake with the remaining white chocolate buttercream, smoothing the sides and top with an offset spatula or bench scraper.
5. Decorate (optional):
    - Garnish the top of the cake with fresh raspberries, white chocolate curls, or edible pearls for an elegant finish.
6. Serve and enjoy!
    - Let the cake sit at room temperature for about 30 minutes before serving to allow the buttercream to soften slightly.

This Raspberry White Chocolate Wedding Cake is a delightful combination of flavors and textures, perfect for celebrating a special wedding day with its elegant presentation and delicious taste.

Pistachio Rose Wedding Cake

Ingredients:

For the pistachio cake:

- 2 cups shelled pistachios, unsalted
- 2 cups cake flour
- 2 teaspoons baking powder
- 1/2 teaspoon baking soda
- 1/2 teaspoon salt
- 1 cup unsalted butter, softened
- 1 1/2 cups granulated sugar
- 4 large eggs
- 1 cup buttermilk
- 1 teaspoon almond extract
- 1 teaspoon vanilla extract
- Green food coloring (optional, for a more vibrant color)

For the rose water syrup:

- 1/2 cup water
- 1/2 cup granulated sugar
- 1 tablespoon rose water

For the pistachio rose buttercream:

- 1 1/2 cups unsalted butter, softened
- 5 cups powdered sugar, sifted
- 1/2 cup shelled pistachios, finely ground
- 2-3 tablespoons rose water (adjust to taste)
- Pink food coloring (optional, for a hint of color)
- Edible rose petals (for decoration, optional)

Instructions:

1. Prepare the pistachio cake:
    - Preheat your oven to 350°F (175°C). Grease and flour three 8-inch round cake pans.
    - In a food processor, pulse the pistachios until finely ground. Be careful not to over-process into a paste.
    - In a medium bowl, whisk together the ground pistachios, cake flour, baking powder, baking soda, and salt.
    - In a large mixing bowl, cream the softened butter and granulated sugar until light and fluffy.
    - Add the eggs one at a time, mixing well after each addition.

- Mix in the buttermilk, almond extract, and vanilla extract until smooth and well combined.
- Gradually add the dry ingredients to the wet ingredients, mixing until just combined.
- If desired, add a few drops of green food coloring to achieve a pistachio color.
- Divide the batter evenly among the prepared cake pans.
- Bake for 25-30 minutes, or until a toothpick inserted into the center of the cakes comes out clean.
- Remove from the oven and let the cakes cool in the pans for 10 minutes. Then, transfer them to a wire rack to cool completely before assembling.

2. Make the rose water syrup:
    - In a small saucepan, combine the water and granulated sugar. Heat over medium heat, stirring until the sugar dissolves.
    - Remove from heat and stir in the rose water. Let the syrup cool completely.

3. Make the pistachio rose buttercream:
    - In a large bowl, beat the softened butter until creamy and smooth.
    - Gradually add the powdered sugar, one cup at a time, beating well after each addition.
    - Mix in the finely ground pistachios and rose water until smooth and fluffy.
    - Add a few drops of pink food coloring, if desired, for a hint of color.
    - Beat on medium-high speed for 3-4 minutes until light and fluffy. Add more rose water if needed to achieve a spreadable consistency.

4. Assemble the cake:
    - Once the cakes are completely cooled, level the tops if necessary using a serrated knife.
    - Place one cake layer on a serving plate or cake stand. Brush a layer of rose water syrup evenly over the top.
    - Spread a layer of pistachio rose buttercream evenly over the top of the first layer.
    - Repeat with the second and third cake layers, brushing syrup and adding buttercream between each layer.
    - Frost the entire cake with a thin layer of buttercream to create a crumb coat. Chill the cake in the refrigerator for 30 minutes to set the crumb coat.
    - Finish frosting the cake with the remaining pistachio rose buttercream, smoothing the sides and top with an offset spatula or bench scraper.

5. Decorate (optional):
    - Garnish the cake with edible rose petals for an elegant touch. You can also sprinkle some finely chopped pistachios on top for added texture and flavor.

6. Serve and enjoy!
    - Let the cake sit at room temperature for about 30 minutes before serving to allow the buttercream to soften slightly.

This Pistachio Rose Wedding Cake is a masterpiece of flavors, combining the nutty crunch of pistachios with the floral essence of rose water. It's sure to impress your guests and make your wedding celebration truly special!

Orange Blossom Wedding Cake

Ingredients:

For the cake:

- 3 cups cake flour
- 1 tablespoon baking powder
- 1/2 teaspoon baking soda
- 1/2 teaspoon salt
- 1 cup unsalted butter, softened
- 2 cups granulated sugar
- 4 large eggs
- 1 cup buttermilk
- 1/2 cup freshly squeezed orange juice
- Zest of 2 oranges
- 1 teaspoon vanilla extract
- 1 teaspoon orange blossom water (optional, for a more pronounced flavor)

For the orange blossom syrup:

- 1/2 cup water
- 1/2 cup granulated sugar
- 1 tablespoon orange blossom water

For the orange blossom buttercream:

- 1 1/2 cups unsalted butter, softened
- 5 cups powdered sugar, sifted
- 1 tablespoon freshly squeezed orange juice
- 1 tablespoon orange blossom water
- Zest of 1 orange
- Orange food coloring (optional, for a hint of color)

Instructions:

1. Prepare the cake:
    - Preheat your oven to 350°F (175°C). Grease and flour three 8-inch round cake pans.
    - In a medium bowl, sift together the cake flour, baking powder, baking soda, and salt.
    - In a large mixing bowl, cream the softened butter and granulated sugar until light and fluffy.
    - Add the eggs one at a time, mixing well after each addition.
    - Mix in the buttermilk, freshly squeezed orange juice, orange zest, vanilla extract, and orange blossom water (if using) until smooth and well combined.

- Gradually add the dry ingredients to the wet ingredients, mixing until just combined.
- Divide the batter evenly among the prepared cake pans.
- Bake for 25-30 minutes, or until a toothpick inserted into the center of the cakes comes out clean.
- Remove from the oven and let the cakes cool in the pans for 10 minutes. Then, transfer them to a wire rack to cool completely before assembling.

2. Make the orange blossom syrup:
    - In a small saucepan, combine the water and granulated sugar. Heat over medium heat, stirring until the sugar dissolves.
    - Remove from heat and stir in the orange blossom water. Let the syrup cool completely.

3. Make the orange blossom buttercream:
    - In a large bowl, beat the softened butter until creamy and smooth.
    - Gradually add the powdered sugar, one cup at a time, beating well after each addition.
    - Mix in the freshly squeezed orange juice, orange blossom water, and orange zest until smooth and fluffy.
    - Add a few drops of orange food coloring, if desired, for a hint of color.
    - Beat on medium-high speed for 3-4 minutes until light and fluffy. Add more orange juice or orange blossom water if needed to achieve a spreadable consistency.

4. Assemble the cake:
    - Once the cakes are completely cooled, level the tops if necessary using a serrated knife.
    - Place one cake layer on a serving plate or cake stand. Brush a layer of orange blossom syrup evenly over the top.
    - Spread a layer of orange blossom buttercream evenly over the top of the first layer.
    - Repeat with the second and third cake layers, brushing syrup and adding buttercream between each layer.
    - Frost the entire cake with a thin layer of buttercream to create a crumb coat. Chill the cake in the refrigerator for 30 minutes to set the crumb coat.
    - Finish frosting the cake with the remaining orange blossom buttercream, smoothing the sides and top with an offset spatula or bench scraper.

5. Decorate (optional):
    - Garnish the cake with fresh orange slices, edible flowers, or orange zest curls for a beautiful presentation.

6. Serve and enjoy!
    - Let the cake sit at room temperature for about 30 minutes before serving to allow the buttercream to soften slightly.

This Orange Blossom Wedding Cake is fragrant, light, and bursting with citrusy flavors, making it a perfect choice for a wedding celebration. It's sure to impress your guests with its delicate aroma and elegant appearance!

Earl Grey Lavender Wedding Cake

Ingredients:

For the Earl Grey Lavender Cake:

- 2 cups cake flour
- 2 teaspoons baking powder
- 1/2 teaspoon baking soda
- 1/2 teaspoon salt
- 1/2 cup unsalted butter, softened
- 1 1/2 cups granulated sugar
- 3 large eggs
- 1/2 cup whole milk
- 1/2 cup sour cream
- 1/4 cup Earl Grey tea leaves (from about 4-5 tea bags or loose leaf)
- 1 tablespoon culinary lavender, finely ground
- Zest of 1 lemon
- 1 teaspoon vanilla extract

For the Earl Grey Lavender Syrup:

- 1/2 cup water
- 1/2 cup granulated sugar
- 2 tablespoons Earl Grey tea leaves
- 1 tablespoon culinary lavender

For the Earl Grey Lavender Buttercream:

- 1 1/2 cups unsalted butter, softened
- 5 cups powdered sugar, sifted
- 1/4 cup Earl Grey tea, brewed and cooled
- 1 tablespoon culinary lavender, finely ground
- Zest of 1 lemon
- Purple food coloring (optional, for a hint of color)

Instructions:

1. Prepare the Earl Grey Lavender Cake:
    - Preheat your oven to 350°F (175°C). Grease and flour three 8-inch round cake pans.
    - In a small saucepan, heat the whole milk until just simmering. Remove from heat and add the Earl Grey tea leaves and culinary lavender. Let steep for 10-15 minutes. Strain the milk mixture through a fine mesh sieve, pressing to extract as much liquid as possible. Set aside to cool.

- In a medium bowl, sift together the cake flour, baking powder, baking soda, and salt.
- In a large mixing bowl, cream the softened butter and granulated sugar until light and fluffy.
- Add the eggs one at a time, mixing well after each addition.
- Mix in the sour cream, strained Earl Grey lavender milk, lemon zest, and vanilla extract until smooth and well combined.
- Gradually add the dry ingredients to the wet ingredients, mixing until just combined.
- Divide the batter evenly among the prepared cake pans.
- Bake for 25-30 minutes, or until a toothpick inserted into the center of the cakes comes out clean.
- Remove from the oven and let the cakes cool in the pans for 10 minutes. Then, transfer them to a wire rack to cool completely before assembling.

2. Make the Earl Grey Lavender Syrup:
    - In a small saucepan, combine the water and granulated sugar. Heat over medium heat, stirring until the sugar dissolves.
    - Add the Earl Grey tea leaves and culinary lavender. Simmer for 5 minutes, then remove from heat and let steep for another 10-15 minutes.
    - Strain the syrup through a fine mesh sieve, pressing to extract as much liquid as possible. Stir in the lemon zest. Let the syrup cool completely.

3. Make the Earl Grey Lavender Buttercream:
    - In a large bowl, beat the softened butter until creamy and smooth.
    - Gradually add the powdered sugar, one cup at a time, beating well after each addition.
    - Mix in the brewed and cooled Earl Grey tea, finely ground culinary lavender, and lemon zest until smooth and fluffy.
    - Add a few drops of purple food coloring, if desired, for a hint of color.
    - Beat on medium-high speed for 3-4 minutes until light and fluffy. Adjust the consistency with more powdered sugar or tea if needed.

4. Assemble the cake:
    - Once the cakes are completely cooled, level the tops if necessary using a serrated knife.
    - Place one cake layer on a serving plate or cake stand. Brush a layer of Earl Grey lavender syrup evenly over the top.
    - Spread a layer of Earl Grey lavender buttercream evenly over the top of the first layer.
    - Repeat with the second and third cake layers, brushing syrup and adding buttercream between each layer.
    - Frost the entire cake with a thin layer of buttercream to create a crumb coat. Chill the cake in the refrigerator for 30 minutes to set the crumb coat.
    - Finish frosting the cake with the remaining Earl Grey lavender buttercream, smoothing the sides and top with an offset spatula or bench scraper.

5. Decorate (optional):

- Garnish the cake with culinary lavender buds or fresh lavender sprigs for a beautiful and aromatic touch.
6. Serve and enjoy!
    - Let the cake sit at room temperature for about 30 minutes before serving to allow the buttercream to soften slightly.

This Earl Grey Lavender Wedding Cake is a sophisticated and aromatic dessert, perfect for a wedding celebration with its delicate floral and tea-infused flavors. It's sure to impress your guests and create a memorable culinary experience!

Coconut Pineapple Wedding Cake

Ingredients:

For the coconut pineapple cake:

- 3 cups cake flour
- 1 tablespoon baking powder
- 1/2 teaspoon baking soda
- 1/2 teaspoon salt
- 1 cup unsalted butter, softened
- 2 cups granulated sugar
- 4 large eggs
- 1 cup coconut milk
- 1 teaspoon vanilla extract
- 1 cup shredded coconut (sweetened or unsweetened)
- 1 cup crushed pineapple, drained well

For the pineapple filling:

- 2 cups crushed pineapple, drained well
- 1/2 cup granulated sugar
- 2 tablespoons cornstarch
- 1 tablespoon lemon juice

For the coconut cream cheese frosting:

- 1 cup unsalted butter, softened
- 12 ounces cream cheese, softened
- 5 cups powdered sugar, sifted
- 1 teaspoon coconut extract
- 1 cup shredded coconut, toasted (for garnish)

Instructions:

1. Prepare the coconut pineapple cake:
    - Preheat your oven to 350°F (175°C). Grease and flour three 8-inch round cake pans.
    - In a medium bowl, sift together the cake flour, baking powder, baking soda, and salt.
    - In a large mixing bowl, cream the softened butter and granulated sugar until light and fluffy.
    - Add the eggs one at a time, mixing well after each addition.
    - Mix in the coconut milk and vanilla extract until smooth and well combined.
    - Gradually add the dry ingredients to the wet ingredients, mixing until just combined.

- Fold in the shredded coconut and crushed pineapple until evenly distributed.
- Divide the batter evenly among the prepared cake pans.
- Bake for 25-30 minutes, or until a toothpick inserted into the center of the cakes comes out clean.
- Remove from the oven and let the cakes cool in the pans for 10 minutes. Then, transfer them to a wire rack to cool completely before assembling.

2. Make the pineapple filling:
   - In a saucepan, combine the drained crushed pineapple, granulated sugar, cornstarch, and lemon juice.
   - Cook over medium heat, stirring constantly, until the mixture thickens and becomes translucent.
   - Remove from heat and let the pineapple filling cool completely.

3. Make the coconut cream cheese frosting:
   - In a large bowl, beat the softened butter and cream cheese until smooth and creamy.
   - Gradually add the powdered sugar, one cup at a time, beating well after each addition.
   - Mix in the coconut extract until smooth and fluffy.

4. Assemble the cake:
   - Once the cakes are completely cooled, level the tops if necessary using a serrated knife.
   - Place one cake layer on a serving plate or cake stand. Spread a layer of coconut cream cheese frosting evenly over the top.
   - Spread a thin layer of pineapple filling over the frosting.
   - Repeat with the second cake layer, more frosting, and pineapple filling, then add the third cake layer on top.
   - Frost the entire cake with a thin layer of coconut cream cheese frosting to create a crumb coat. Chill the cake in the refrigerator for 30 minutes to set the crumb coat.
   - Finish frosting the cake with the remaining coconut cream cheese frosting, smoothing the sides and top with an offset spatula or bench scraper.

5. Decorate (optional):
   - Garnish the top of the cake with toasted shredded coconut for added texture and a tropical look.

6. Serve and enjoy!
   - Let the cake sit at room temperature for about 30 minutes before serving to allow the frosting to soften slightly.

This Coconut Pineapple Wedding Cake is a tropical delight, combining the flavors of coconut and pineapple for a refreshing and delicious dessert that's perfect for celebrating a special wedding day, especially in a warm and sunny setting.

Marble Wedding Cake

Ingredients:

For the vanilla cake batter:

- 2 cups cake flour
- 2 teaspoons baking powder
- 1/2 teaspoon baking soda
- 1/2 teaspoon salt
- 1 cup unsalted butter, softened
- 1 1/2 cups granulated sugar
- 4 large eggs
- 1 cup buttermilk
- 1 teaspoon vanilla extract

For the chocolate cake batter:

- 1 1/2 cups cake flour
- 1/2 cup unsweetened cocoa powder
- 2 teaspoons baking powder
- 1/2 teaspoon baking soda
- 1/2 teaspoon salt
- 1 cup unsalted butter, softened
- 1 1/2 cups granulated sugar
- 4 large eggs
- 1 cup buttermilk
- 1 teaspoon vanilla extract

For the marble effect:

- 1/2 cup hot water
- 2 tablespoons instant coffee or espresso powder (optional, for a deeper marble effect)
- 1/4 cup unsweetened cocoa powder

For the vanilla buttercream:

- 2 cups unsalted butter, softened
- 6 cups powdered sugar, sifted
- 2 teaspoons vanilla extract
- 4-6 tablespoons heavy cream or milk

Instructions:

1. Prepare the vanilla cake batter:

- Preheat your oven to 350°F (175°C). Grease and flour three 8-inch round cake pans.
- In a medium bowl, sift together the cake flour, baking powder, baking soda, and salt.
- In a large mixing bowl, cream the softened butter and granulated sugar until light and fluffy.
- Add the eggs one at a time, mixing well after each addition.
- Mix in the buttermilk and vanilla extract until smooth and well combined.
- Gradually add the dry ingredients to the wet ingredients, mixing until just combined.
- Set aside.

2. Prepare the chocolate cake batter:
    - In another medium bowl, sift together the cake flour, cocoa powder, baking powder, baking soda, and salt.
    - In a large mixing bowl, cream the softened butter and granulated sugar until light and fluffy.
    - Add the eggs one at a time, mixing well after each addition.
    - Mix in the buttermilk and vanilla extract until smooth and well combined.
    - Gradually add the dry ingredients to the wet ingredients, mixing until just combined.
    - Set aside.

3. Create the marble effect:
    - In a small bowl, mix the hot water with instant coffee or espresso powder (if using).
    - Divide the vanilla cake batter into two portions.
    - Mix the cocoa powder into one portion of the vanilla cake batter until well combined.
    - Pour dollops of each batter alternately into the prepared cake pans.
    - Use a butter knife or skewer to swirl the batters together gently, creating a marbled effect.

4. Bake the cakes:
    - Bake in the preheated oven for 25-30 minutes, or until a toothpick inserted into the center of the cakes comes out clean.
    - Remove from the oven and let the cakes cool in the pans for 10 minutes. Then, transfer them to a wire rack to cool completely before assembling.

5. Prepare the vanilla buttercream:
    - In a large bowl, beat the softened butter until creamy and smooth.
    - Gradually add the powdered sugar, one cup at a time, beating well after each addition.
    - Mix in the vanilla extract.
    - Add heavy cream or milk, one tablespoon at a time, until the desired consistency is reached. Beat on medium-high speed for 3-4 minutes until light and fluffy.

6. Assemble the cake:

- Once the cakes are completely cooled, level the tops if necessary using a serrated knife.
- Place one cake layer on a serving plate or cake stand.
- Spread a layer of vanilla buttercream evenly over the top.
- Add the next cake layer and repeat with more buttercream.
- Add the final cake layer on top, ensuring the marbled side is facing up.
- Frost the entire cake with a thin layer of buttercream to create a crumb coat. Chill the cake in the refrigerator for 30 minutes to set the crumb coat.
- Finish frosting the cake with the remaining vanilla buttercream, smoothing the sides and top with an offset spatula or bench scraper.

7. Decorate (optional):
   - You can leave the cake with its marbled effect for a simple and elegant look, or decorate with chocolate curls, sprinkles, or fresh flowers for a more festive appearance.
8. Serve and enjoy!
   - Let the cake sit at room temperature for about 30 minutes before serving to allow the buttercream to soften slightly.

This Marble Wedding Cake is sure to impress with its beautiful marbled pattern and delicious combination of vanilla and chocolate flavors. It's a timeless choice that will be enjoyed by all at your wedding celebration!

Carrot Cake with Cream Cheese Frosting

Ingredients:

For the carrot cake:

- 2 cups all-purpose flour
- 2 teaspoons baking powder
- 1 1/2 teaspoons baking soda
- 1 teaspoon salt
- 2 teaspoons ground cinnamon
- 1/2 teaspoon ground nutmeg
- 1/2 teaspoon ground ginger
- 1 cup vegetable oil
- 1 cup granulated sugar
- 1 cup brown sugar, packed
- 4 large eggs
- 2 teaspoons vanilla extract
- 3 cups grated carrots (about 4-5 medium carrots)
- 1 cup crushed pineapple, drained well
- 1 cup shredded coconut (sweetened or unsweetened)
- 1 cup chopped walnuts or pecans (optional)

For the cream cheese frosting:

- 1 cup unsalted butter, softened
- 16 ounces cream cheese, softened
- 4 cups powdered sugar, sifted
- 2 teaspoons vanilla extract

Instructions:

1. Prepare the carrot cake:
    - Preheat your oven to 350°F (175°C). Grease and flour three 8-inch round cake pans, or you can use parchment paper for easier removal.
    - In a large bowl, sift together the flour, baking powder, baking soda, salt, cinnamon, nutmeg, and ginger.
    - In another large mixing bowl, whisk together the vegetable oil, granulated sugar, brown sugar, eggs, and vanilla extract until well combined.
    - Gradually add the dry ingredients to the wet ingredients, mixing until just combined.
    - Fold in the grated carrots, crushed pineapple, shredded coconut, and chopped nuts (if using), until evenly distributed.
    - Divide the batter evenly among the prepared cake pans.

- Bake for 25-30 minutes, or until a toothpick inserted into the center of the cakes comes out clean.
- Remove from the oven and let the cakes cool in the pans for 10 minutes. Then, transfer them to a wire rack to cool completely before frosting.

2. Make the cream cheese frosting:
    - In a large bowl, beat the softened butter and cream cheese until smooth and creamy.
    - Gradually add the powdered sugar, one cup at a time, beating well after each addition.
    - Mix in the vanilla extract until smooth and fluffy. Beat on medium-high speed for 3-4 minutes until light and creamy.

3. Assemble the cake:
    - Once the cakes are completely cooled, level the tops if necessary using a serrated knife.
    - Place one cake layer on a serving plate or cake stand.
    - Spread a layer of cream cheese frosting evenly over the top.
    - Add the next cake layer and repeat with more frosting.
    - Add the final cake layer on top.
    - Frost the entire cake with a thin layer of cream cheese frosting to create a crumb coat. Chill the cake in the refrigerator for 30 minutes to set the crumb coat.
    - Finish frosting the cake with the remaining cream cheese frosting, smoothing the sides and top with an offset spatula or bench scraper.

4. Decorate (optional):
    - Garnish the cake with chopped nuts, shredded coconut, or carrot decorations on top for a beautiful presentation.

5. Serve and enjoy!
    - Let the cake sit at room temperature for about 30 minutes before serving to allow the frosting to soften slightly.

This Carrot Cake with Cream Cheese Frosting is moist, flavorful, and perfect for any wedding or special occasion. It's sure to be a hit with its rich carrot flavor and creamy frosting!

Mint Chocolate Chip Wedding Cake

Ingredients:

For the chocolate cake:

- 2 cups all-purpose flour
- 1 cup unsweetened cocoa powder
- 2 teaspoons baking powder
- 1 1/2 teaspoons baking soda
- 1 teaspoon salt
- 2 cups granulated sugar
- 1 cup vegetable oil
- 4 large eggs
- 2 teaspoons vanilla extract
- 1 cup buttermilk
- 1 cup boiling water

For the mint frosting:

- 1 1/2 cups unsalted butter, softened
- 6 cups powdered sugar, sifted
- 1 teaspoon peppermint extract
- Green food coloring (optional)
- 1/2 cup mini chocolate chips (for decoration and flavor)

Instructions:

1. Prepare the chocolate cake:
    - Preheat your oven to 350°F (175°C). Grease and flour three 8-inch round cake pans.
    - In a large mixing bowl, sift together the flour, cocoa powder, baking powder, baking soda, and salt.
    - In another large bowl, whisk together the granulated sugar, vegetable oil, eggs, and vanilla extract until well combined.
    - Gradually add the dry ingredients to the wet ingredients, alternating with the buttermilk, mixing on low speed until just combined.
    - Carefully add the boiling water to the batter, mixing until smooth (batter will be thin).
    - Divide the batter evenly among the prepared cake pans.
    - Bake for 30-35 minutes, or until a toothpick inserted into the center of the cakes comes out clean.
    - Remove from the oven and let the cakes cool in the pans for 10 minutes. Then, transfer them to a wire rack to cool completely before frosting.
2. Make the mint frosting:

- In a large bowl, beat the softened butter until creamy and smooth.
- Gradually add the powdered sugar, one cup at a time, beating well after each addition.
- Mix in the peppermint extract and green food coloring (if using), until desired mint flavor and color are achieved.
- Beat on medium-high speed for 3-4 minutes until light and fluffy.

3. Assemble the cake:
    - Once the cakes are completely cooled, level the tops if necessary using a serrated knife.
    - Place one cake layer on a serving plate or cake stand.
    - Spread a layer of mint frosting evenly over the top.
    - Sprinkle a generous amount of mini chocolate chips over the frosting.
    - Repeat with the next cake layer, more frosting, and chocolate chips.
    - Add the final cake layer on top.
    - Frost the entire cake with a thin layer of mint frosting to create a crumb coat. Chill the cake in the refrigerator for 30 minutes to set the crumb coat.
    - Finish frosting the cake with the remaining mint frosting, smoothing the sides and top with an offset spatula or bench scraper.

4. Decorate (optional):
    - Garnish the top of the cake with additional mini chocolate chips for a decorative touch.

5. Serve and enjoy!
    - Let the cake sit at room temperature for about 30 minutes before serving to allow the frosting to soften slightly.

This Mint Chocolate Chip Wedding Cake combines the cool freshness of mint with the indulgence of chocolate, making it a delightful and memorable dessert for your special day. It's sure to impress your guests with its unique flavor and beautiful presentation!

Matcha Green Tea Wedding Cake

Ingredients:

For the matcha green tea cake:

- 2 1/2 cups cake flour
- 2 teaspoons baking powder
- 1/2 teaspoon baking soda
- 1/2 teaspoon salt
- 1 tablespoon matcha green tea powder
- 1 cup unsalted butter, softened
- 1 1/2 cups granulated sugar
- 4 large eggs
- 1 cup buttermilk
- 1 teaspoon vanilla extract

For the matcha green tea buttercream:

- 1 1/2 cups unsalted butter, softened
- 6 cups powdered sugar, sifted
- 2 tablespoons matcha green tea powder
- 1-2 tablespoons heavy cream or milk

Instructions:

1. Prepare the matcha green tea cake:
    - Preheat your oven to 350°F (175°C). Grease and flour three 8-inch round cake pans.
    - In a medium bowl, sift together the cake flour, baking powder, baking soda, salt, and matcha green tea powder.
    - In a large mixing bowl, cream the softened butter and granulated sugar until light and fluffy.
    - Add the eggs one at a time, mixing well after each addition.
    - Mix in the buttermilk and vanilla extract until smooth and well combined.
    - Gradually add the dry ingredients to the wet ingredients, mixing until just combined.
    - Divide the batter evenly among the prepared cake pans.
    - Bake for 25-30 minutes, or until a toothpick inserted into the center of the cakes comes out clean.
    - Remove from the oven and let the cakes cool in the pans for 10 minutes. Then, transfer them to a wire rack to cool completely before frosting.
2. Make the matcha green tea buttercream:
    - In a large bowl, beat the softened butter until creamy and smooth.

- Gradually add the powdered sugar, one cup at a time, beating well after each addition.
- Mix in the matcha green tea powder until well incorporated.
- Add heavy cream or milk, one tablespoon at a time, until the frosting reaches your desired consistency. Beat on medium-high speed for 3-4 minutes until light and fluffy.

3. Assemble the cake:
   - Once the cakes are completely cooled, level the tops if necessary using a serrated knife.
   - Place one cake layer on a serving plate or cake stand.
   - Spread a layer of matcha green tea buttercream evenly over the top.
   - Add the next cake layer and repeat with more buttercream.
   - Add the final cake layer on top.
   - Frost the entire cake with a thin layer of matcha green tea buttercream to create a crumb coat. Chill the cake in the refrigerator for 30 minutes to set the crumb coat.
   - Finish frosting the cake with the remaining matcha green tea buttercream, smoothing the sides and top with an offset spatula or bench scraper.

4. Decorate (optional):
   - Garnish the top of the cake with sifted matcha green tea powder for a decorative finish.
   - You can also add edible flowers, fresh berries, or chocolate decorations as desired.

5. Serve and enjoy!
   - Let the cake sit at room temperature for about 30 minutes before serving to allow the buttercream to soften slightly.

This Matcha Green Tea Wedding Cake is not only visually stunning with its vibrant green color but also offers a distinctively earthy and slightly bitter-sweet flavor profile that will delight guests looking for something unique and sophisticated at your wedding celebration.

Tiramisu Wedding Cake

Ingredients:

For the cake:

- 2 cups cake flour
- 2 teaspoons baking powder
- 1/2 teaspoon baking soda
- 1/2 teaspoon salt
- 1/2 cup unsalted butter, softened
- 1 cup granulated sugar
- 3 large eggs
- 1 teaspoon vanilla extract
- 1/2 cup buttermilk
- 1/2 cup brewed espresso or strong coffee, cooled

For the coffee syrup:

- 1/2 cup brewed espresso or strong coffee, cooled
- 2 tablespoons coffee liqueur (optional)
- 2 tablespoons granulated sugar

For the mascarpone filling:

- 16 ounces mascarpone cheese, softened
- 1 cup powdered sugar, sifted
- 1 cup heavy cream, chilled
- 1 teaspoon vanilla extract

For the topping:

- Cocoa powder, for dusting
- Chocolate shavings or curls, for garnish

Instructions:

1. Prepare the cake:
   - Preheat your oven to 350°F (175°C). Grease and flour three 8-inch round cake pans.
   - In a medium bowl, sift together the cake flour, baking powder, baking soda, and salt.
   - In a large mixing bowl, cream the softened butter and granulated sugar until light and fluffy.
   - Add the eggs one at a time, mixing well after each addition.
   - Mix in the vanilla extract.

- Gradually add the dry ingredients to the wet ingredients, alternating with the buttermilk and brewed espresso, mixing until just combined.
- Divide the batter evenly among the prepared cake pans.
- Bake for 25-30 minutes, or until a toothpick inserted into the center of the cakes comes out clean.
- Remove from the oven and let the cakes cool in the pans for 10 minutes. Then, transfer them to a wire rack to cool completely.

2. Make the coffee syrup:
   - In a small bowl, combine the brewed espresso (or strong coffee), coffee liqueur (if using), and granulated sugar. Stir until the sugar is dissolved. Set aside to cool.

3. Prepare the mascarpone filling:
   - In a mixing bowl, beat the mascarpone cheese until smooth and creamy.
   - Gradually add the powdered sugar, beating until well combined.
   - In a separate bowl, whip the chilled heavy cream and vanilla extract until stiff peaks form.
   - Gently fold the whipped cream into the mascarpone mixture until smooth and well combined. Refrigerate until ready to assemble the cake.

4. Assemble the cake:
   - Once the cakes are completely cooled, level the tops if necessary using a serrated knife.
   - Place one cake layer on a serving plate or cake stand.
   - Brush the top of the cake layer with a generous amount of coffee syrup.
   - Spread a layer of mascarpone filling evenly over the soaked cake layer.
   - Repeat with the next cake layer, more coffee syrup, and mascarpone filling.
   - Add the final cake layer on top.
   - Frost the entire cake with a thin layer of mascarpone filling to create a crumb coat. Chill the cake in the refrigerator for 30 minutes to set the crumb coat.
   - Finish frosting the cake with the remaining mascarpone filling, smoothing the sides and top with an offset spatula or bench scraper.

5. Decorate:
   - Dust the top of the cake with cocoa powder using a fine-mesh sieve.
   - Garnish with chocolate shavings or curls for an elegant finish.

6. Chill and serve:
   - Refrigerate the Tiramisu Wedding Cake for at least 4 hours, preferably overnight, to allow the flavors to meld and the cake to set.
   - Slice and serve chilled for the best texture and taste.

This Tiramisu Wedding Cake is a decadent and sophisticated choice, perfect for coffee and dessert lovers alike. Its layers of espresso-soaked cake and creamy mascarpone filling create a memorable dessert that will impress your wedding guests with its rich flavors and elegant presentation.

Ginger Spice Wedding Cake

Ingredients:

For the cake:

- 3 cups cake flour
- 1 tablespoon ground ginger
- 1 1/2 teaspoons ground cinnamon
- 1/2 teaspoon ground nutmeg
- 1/2 teaspoon ground cloves
- 1/2 teaspoon ground allspice
- 1 teaspoon baking powder
- 1/2 teaspoon baking soda
- 1/2 teaspoon salt
- 1 cup unsalted butter, softened
- 1 cup granulated sugar
- 1 cup brown sugar, packed
- 4 large eggs
- 1 cup buttermilk
- 1/2 cup molasses
- 1 tablespoon vanilla extract

For the cream cheese frosting:

- 1 cup unsalted butter, softened
- 16 ounces cream cheese, softened
- 6 cups powdered sugar, sifted
- 2 teaspoons vanilla extract

Instructions:

1. Prepare the cake:
    - Preheat your oven to 350°F (175°C). Grease and flour three 8-inch round cake pans.
    - In a large bowl, sift together the cake flour, ground ginger, cinnamon, nutmeg, cloves, allspice, baking powder, baking soda, and salt.
    - In another large mixing bowl, cream the softened butter, granulated sugar, and brown sugar until light and fluffy.
    - Add the eggs one at a time, mixing well after each addition.
    - Mix in the buttermilk, molasses, and vanilla extract until smooth and well combined.
    - Gradually add the dry ingredients to the wet ingredients, mixing until just combined.
    - Divide the batter evenly among the prepared cake pans.

- Bake for 25-30 minutes, or until a toothpick inserted into the center of the cakes comes out clean.
- Remove from the oven and let the cakes cool in the pans for 10 minutes. Then, transfer them to a wire rack to cool completely before frosting.

2. Make the cream cheese frosting:
    - In a large bowl, beat the softened butter and cream cheese until smooth and creamy.
    - Gradually add the powdered sugar, one cup at a time, beating well after each addition.
    - Mix in the vanilla extract until smooth and fluffy. Beat on medium-high speed for 3-4 minutes until light and creamy.
3. Assemble the cake:
    - Once the cakes are completely cooled, level the tops if necessary using a serrated knife.
    - Place one cake layer on a serving plate or cake stand.
    - Spread a layer of cream cheese frosting evenly over the top.
    - Add the next cake layer and repeat with more frosting.
    - Add the final cake layer on top.
    - Frost the entire cake with a thin layer of cream cheese frosting to create a crumb coat. Chill the cake in the refrigerator for 30 minutes to set the crumb coat.
    - Finish frosting the cake with the remaining cream cheese frosting, smoothing the sides and top with an offset spatula or bench scraper.
4. Decorate (optional):
    - Garnish the top of the cake with crystallized ginger pieces or a sprinkle of ground cinnamon for an extra touch of flavor and decoration.
5. Serve and enjoy!
    - Let the cake sit at room temperature for about 30 minutes before serving to allow the frosting to soften slightly.

This Ginger Spice Wedding Cake is rich in warm spices and complemented perfectly by the creamy tang of the cream cheese frosting. It's a delicious and festive dessert choice that will add warmth and flavor to your wedding celebration!

Caramel Apple Wedding Cake

Ingredients:

For the cake:

- 3 cups all-purpose flour
- 2 teaspoons baking powder
- 1/2 teaspoon baking soda
- 1/2 teaspoon salt
- 1 teaspoon ground cinnamon
- 1/2 teaspoon ground nutmeg
- 1/4 teaspoon ground cloves
- 1 cup unsalted butter, softened
- 1 cup granulated sugar
- 1 cup brown sugar, packed
- 4 large eggs
- 2 teaspoons vanilla extract
- 1 cup buttermilk
- 2 cups finely chopped apples (peeled and cored)

For the caramel sauce:

- 1 cup granulated sugar
- 6 tablespoons unsalted butter, cut into pieces
- 1/2 cup heavy cream
- Pinch of salt

For the cream cheese frosting:

- 1 cup unsalted butter, softened
- 16 ounces cream cheese, softened
- 6 cups powdered sugar, sifted
- 2 teaspoons vanilla extract

Instructions:

1. Prepare the cake:
   - Preheat your oven to 350°F (175°C). Grease and flour three 8-inch round cake pans.
   - In a medium bowl, sift together the flour, baking powder, baking soda, salt, cinnamon, nutmeg, and cloves.
   - In a large mixing bowl, cream the softened butter, granulated sugar, and brown sugar until light and fluffy.
   - Add the eggs one at a time, mixing well after each addition.
   - Mix in the vanilla extract.

- Gradually add the dry ingredients to the wet ingredients, alternating with the buttermilk, mixing until just combined.
- Fold in the finely chopped apples until evenly distributed.
- Divide the batter evenly among the prepared cake pans.
- Bake for 25-30 minutes, or until a toothpick inserted into the center of the cakes comes out clean.
- Remove from the oven and let the cakes cool in the pans for 10 minutes. Then, transfer them to a wire rack to cool completely before frosting.

2. Make the caramel sauce:
    - In a medium saucepan, heat the granulated sugar over medium-high heat, stirring constantly with a heat-resistant spatula or wooden spoon.
    - The sugar will form clumps and eventually melt into a thick, amber-colored liquid as you continue to stir. Be careful not to burn it.
    - Once the sugar is completely melted, add the butter. The mixture will bubble rapidly - be cautious.
    - Stir the butter into the caramel until it is completely melted, about 2-3 minutes.
    - Slowly drizzle in the heavy cream while stirring continuously. Be careful as the mixture will bubble vigorously.
    - Allow the caramel to boil for 1 minute, then remove from heat and stir in the salt.
    - Let the caramel sauce cool to room temperature before using.

3. Make the cream cheese frosting:
    - In a large bowl, beat the softened butter and cream cheese until smooth and creamy.
    - Gradually add the powdered sugar, one cup at a time, beating well after each addition.
    - Mix in the vanilla extract until smooth and fluffy. Beat on medium-high speed for 3-4 minutes until light and creamy.

4. Assemble the cake:
    - Once the cakes are completely cooled, level the tops if necessary using a serrated knife.
    - Place one cake layer on a serving plate or cake stand.
    - Drizzle a generous amount of caramel sauce over the cake layer.
    - Spread a layer of cream cheese frosting evenly over the caramel sauce.
    - Repeat with the next cake layer, more caramel sauce, and cream cheese frosting.
    - Add the final cake layer on top.
    - Frost the entire cake with a thin layer of cream cheese frosting to create a crumb coat. Chill the cake in the refrigerator for 30 minutes to set the crumb coat.
    - Finish frosting the cake with the remaining cream cheese frosting, smoothing the sides and top with an offset spatula or bench scraper.

5. Decorate (optional):
    - Drizzle additional caramel sauce over the top of the cake for a decorative touch.
    - Garnish with apple slices, caramel candies, or chopped nuts if desired.

6. Serve and enjoy!

- Let the cake sit at room temperature for about 30 minutes before serving to allow the frosting to soften slightly.

This Caramel Apple Wedding Cake is a delightful combination of moist apple cake layers, creamy caramel sauce, and tangy cream cheese frosting. It's sure to be a hit at any wedding celebration with its rich flavors and beautiful presentation!

Black Forest Wedding Cake

Ingredients:

For the chocolate cake:

- 2 cups all-purpose flour
- 1 cup unsweetened cocoa powder
- 2 teaspoons baking powder
- 1 1/2 teaspoons baking soda
- 1 teaspoon salt
- 2 cups granulated sugar
- 1 cup vegetable oil
- 4 large eggs
- 2 teaspoons vanilla extract
- 1 cup buttermilk
- 1 cup hot water

For the cherry filling:

- 4 cups pitted cherries (fresh or canned, drained)
- 1/2 cup granulated sugar
- 2 tablespoons cornstarch
- 1/4 cup water
- 1 tablespoon lemon juice
- 1 teaspoon vanilla extract

For the whipped cream frosting:

- 4 cups heavy cream, chilled
- 1 cup powdered sugar, sifted
- 2 teaspoons vanilla extract

For assembly and decoration:

- 1 cup cherry liqueur (optional)
- Chocolate shavings or curls, for garnish
- Fresh cherries, for garnish (optional)

Instructions:

1. Prepare the chocolate cake:
    - Preheat your oven to 350°F (175°C). Grease and flour three 8-inch round cake pans.
    - In a large bowl, sift together the flour, cocoa powder, baking powder, baking soda, and salt.

- In another large mixing bowl, whisk together the granulated sugar, vegetable oil, eggs, and vanilla extract until well combined.
- Gradually add the dry ingredients to the wet ingredients, alternating with the buttermilk, mixing until just combined.
- Carefully add the hot water to the batter, mixing until smooth (batter will be thin).
- Divide the batter evenly among the prepared cake pans.
- Bake for 25-30 minutes, or until a toothpick inserted into the center of the cakes comes out clean.
- Remove from the oven and let the cakes cool in the pans for 10 minutes. Then, transfer them to a wire rack to cool completely.

2. Make the cherry filling:
    - In a medium saucepan, combine the pitted cherries, granulated sugar, and water.
    - Bring to a simmer over medium heat, stirring occasionally.
    - In a small bowl, mix together the cornstarch, lemon juice, and vanilla extract until smooth.
    - Gradually stir the cornstarch mixture into the simmering cherry mixture.
    - Cook, stirring constantly, until the mixture thickens and becomes glossy (about 2-3 minutes).
    - Remove from heat and let cool completely before using.
3. Make the whipped cream frosting:
    - In a large mixing bowl, beat the chilled heavy cream, powdered sugar, and vanilla extract until stiff peaks form.
4. Assemble the cake:
    - Once the cakes are completely cooled, level the tops if necessary using a serrated knife.
    - Place one cake layer on a serving plate or cake stand.
    - If using, brush the top of the cake layer with cherry liqueur for added flavor (optional).
    - Spread a layer of whipped cream frosting evenly over the cake layer.
    - Spoon a generous amount of cherry filling over the whipped cream frosting, spreading evenly.
    - Add the next cake layer on top and repeat with more whipped cream frosting and cherry filling.
    - Add the final cake layer on top.
    - Frost the entire cake with a thin layer of whipped cream frosting to create a crumb coat. Chill the cake in the refrigerator for 30 minutes to set the crumb coat.
    - Finish frosting the cake with the remaining whipped cream frosting, smoothing the sides and top with an offset spatula or bench scraper.
5. Decorate:
    - Garnish the top of the cake with chocolate shavings or curls for an elegant finish.
    - Add fresh cherries on top for decoration, if desired.
6. Serve and enjoy!

- Refrigerate the Black Forest Wedding Cake until ready to serve. Let the cake sit at room temperature for about 30 minutes before serving to allow the frosting to soften slightly.

This Black Forest Wedding Cake is a decadent combination of chocolate, cherries, and whipped cream, making it a luxurious and delightful choice for celebrating a special occasion like a wedding. It's sure to impress with its rich flavors and beautiful presentation!

Cookies and Cream Wedding Cake

Ingredients:

For the chocolate cake:

- 2 cups all-purpose flour
- 1 cup unsweetened cocoa powder
- 2 teaspoons baking powder
- 1 1/2 teaspoons baking soda
- 1 teaspoon salt
- 2 cups granulated sugar
- 1 cup vegetable oil
- 4 large eggs
- 2 teaspoons vanilla extract
- 1 cup buttermilk
- 1 cup hot water

For the cookies and cream filling:

- 20 chocolate sandwich cookies (like Oreo), crushed into small pieces
- 2 cups heavy cream, chilled
- 1/2 cup powdered sugar, sifted
- 1 teaspoon vanilla extract

For the cookies and cream frosting:

- 1 cup unsalted butter, softened
- 8 ounces cream cheese, softened
- 5 cups powdered sugar, sifted
- 2 teaspoons vanilla extract
- 12 chocolate sandwich cookies (like Oreo), crushed into fine crumbs (for decoration)

Instructions:

1. Prepare the chocolate cake:
    - Preheat your oven to 350°F (175°C). Grease and flour three 8-inch round cake pans.
    - In a large bowl, sift together the flour, cocoa powder, baking powder, baking soda, and salt.
    - In another large mixing bowl, whisk together the granulated sugar, vegetable oil, eggs, and vanilla extract until well combined.
    - Gradually add the dry ingredients to the wet ingredients, alternating with the buttermilk, mixing until just combined.
    - Carefully add the hot water to the batter, mixing until smooth (batter will be thin).
    - Divide the batter evenly among the prepared cake pans.

- Bake for 25-30 minutes, or until a toothpick inserted into the center of the cakes comes out clean.
- Remove from the oven and let the cakes cool in the pans for 10 minutes. Then, transfer them to a wire rack to cool completely.

2. Make the cookies and cream filling:
   - In a mixing bowl, beat the chilled heavy cream, powdered sugar, and vanilla extract until stiff peaks form.
   - Gently fold in the crushed chocolate sandwich cookies until evenly distributed. Set aside.

3. Make the cookies and cream frosting:
   - In a large mixing bowl, beat the softened butter and cream cheese until smooth and creamy.
   - Gradually add the powdered sugar, one cup at a time, beating well after each addition.
   - Mix in the vanilla extract until smooth and fluffy. Beat on medium-high speed for 3-4 minutes until light and creamy.
   - Gently fold in the crushed chocolate sandwich cookies until evenly distributed.

4. Assemble the cake:
   - Once the cakes are completely cooled, level the tops if necessary using a serrated knife.
   - Place one cake layer on a serving plate or cake stand.
   - Spread a layer of cookies and cream filling evenly over the cake layer.
   - Add the next cake layer on top and repeat with more filling.
   - Add the final cake layer on top.
   - Frost the entire cake with a thin layer of cookies and cream frosting to create a crumb coat. Chill the cake in the refrigerator for 30 minutes to set the crumb coat.
   - Finish frosting the cake with the remaining cookies and cream frosting, smoothing the sides and top with an offset spatula or bench scraper.

5. Decorate:
   - Sprinkle the top of the cake with the remaining crushed chocolate sandwich cookies for decoration.

6. Serve and enjoy!
   - Refrigerate the Cookies and Cream Wedding Cake until ready to serve. Let the cake sit at room temperature for about 30 minutes before serving to allow the frosting to soften slightly.

This Cookies and Cream Wedding Cake is sure to be a hit with its rich chocolate cake layers, creamy cookies and cream filling, and decadent cookies and cream frosting. It's perfect for any wedding celebration, combining classic flavors with a beautiful presentation!

Pina Colada Wedding Cake

Ingredients:

For the cake:

- 3 cups cake flour
- 1 tablespoon baking powder
- 1/2 teaspoon baking soda
- 1/2 teaspoon salt
- 1 cup unsalted butter, softened
- 2 cups granulated sugar
- 4 large eggs
- 1 teaspoon vanilla extract
- 1 cup coconut milk
- 1/2 cup pineapple juice
- 1 cup shredded coconut (sweetened or unsweetened, depending on your preference)
- 1/2 cup crushed pineapple (well-drained)

For the pineapple-coconut filling:

- 1 cup crushed pineapple (well-drained)
- 1 cup shredded coconut (sweetened or unsweetened)
- 1/2 cup granulated sugar
- 2 tablespoons cornstarch
- 1/4 cup water
- 1 tablespoon lemon juice

For the coconut cream cheese frosting:

- 1 cup unsalted butter, softened
- 16 ounces cream cheese, softened
- 4 cups powdered sugar, sifted
- 1 teaspoon vanilla extract
- 1 teaspoon coconut extract (optional, for extra coconut flavor)

Instructions:

1. Prepare the cake:
    - Preheat your oven to 350°F (175°C). Grease and flour three 8-inch round cake pans.
    - In a medium bowl, sift together the cake flour, baking powder, baking soda, and salt.
    - In a large mixing bowl, cream the softened butter and granulated sugar until light and fluffy.
    - Add the eggs one at a time, mixing well after each addition.

- Mix in the vanilla extract.
- In a separate bowl, combine the coconut milk and pineapple juice.
- Gradually add the dry ingredients to the creamed mixture, alternating with the coconut milk and pineapple juice mixture, mixing until just combined.
- Fold in the shredded coconut and crushed pineapple until evenly distributed.
- Divide the batter evenly among the prepared cake pans.
- Bake for 25-30 minutes, or until a toothpick inserted into the center of the cakes comes out clean.
- Remove from the oven and let the cakes cool in the pans for 10 minutes. Then, transfer them to a wire rack to cool completely before frosting.

2. Make the pineapple-coconut filling:
   - In a medium saucepan, combine the crushed pineapple, shredded coconut, granulated sugar, cornstarch, water, and lemon juice.
   - Cook over medium heat, stirring constantly, until the mixture thickens and becomes glossy (about 5-7 minutes).
   - Remove from heat and let cool completely before using.

3. Make the coconut cream cheese frosting:
   - In a large mixing bowl, beat the softened butter and cream cheese until smooth and creamy.
   - Gradually add the powdered sugar, one cup at a time, beating well after each addition.
   - Mix in the vanilla extract and coconut extract (if using) until smooth and fluffy. Beat on medium-high speed for 3-4 minutes until light and creamy.

4. Assemble the cake:
   - Once the cakes are completely cooled, level the tops if necessary using a serrated knife.
   - Place one cake layer on a serving plate or cake stand.
   - Spread a layer of pineapple-coconut filling evenly over the cake layer.
   - Add the next cake layer on top and repeat with more filling.
   - Add the final cake layer on top.
   - Frost the entire cake with a thin layer of coconut cream cheese frosting to create a crumb coat. Chill the cake in the refrigerator for 30 minutes to set the crumb coat.
   - Finish frosting the cake with the remaining coconut cream cheese frosting, smoothing the sides and top with an offset spatula or bench scraper.

5. Decorate (optional):
   - Garnish the top of the cake with toasted coconut flakes for an extra touch of texture and flavor.
   - Optionally, decorate with fresh pineapple slices or maraschino cherries for a tropical flair.

6. Serve and enjoy!
   - Refrigerate the Pina Colada Wedding Cake until ready to serve. Let the cake sit at room temperature for about 30 minutes before serving to allow the frosting to soften slightly.

This Pina Colada Wedding Cake is a tropical paradise in dessert form, with moist coconut-pineapple cake layers, luscious pineapple-coconut filling, and creamy coconut cream cheese frosting. It's a perfect choice for a wedding celebration, bringing a taste of the tropics to your special day!

Pumpkin Spice Wedding Cake

Ingredients:

For the cake:

- 3 cups all-purpose flour
- 2 teaspoons baking powder
- 1 teaspoon baking soda
- 1/2 teaspoon salt
- 2 teaspoons ground cinnamon
- 1/2 teaspoon ground nutmeg
- 1/2 teaspoon ground ginger
- 1/4 teaspoon ground cloves
- 1 cup unsalted butter, softened
- 2 cups granulated sugar
- 4 large eggs
- 1 can (15 ounces) pumpkin puree (not pumpkin pie filling)
- 1/2 cup buttermilk
- 1 teaspoon vanilla extract

For the cream cheese frosting:

- 1 cup unsalted butter, softened
- 16 ounces cream cheese, softened
- 6 cups powdered sugar, sifted
- 2 teaspoons vanilla extract

Instructions:

1. Prepare the cake:
    - Preheat your oven to 350°F (175°C). Grease and flour three 8-inch round cake pans.
    - In a medium bowl, sift together the flour, baking powder, baking soda, salt, cinnamon, nutmeg, ginger, and cloves.
    - In a large mixing bowl, cream the softened butter and granulated sugar until light and fluffy.
    - Add the eggs one at a time, mixing well after each addition.
    - Mix in the pumpkin puree until well combined.
    - Gradually add the dry ingredients to the wet ingredients, alternating with the buttermilk, mixing until just combined.
    - Stir in the vanilla extract until smooth.
    - Divide the batter evenly among the prepared cake pans.
    - Bake for 25-30 minutes, or until a toothpick inserted into the center of the cakes comes out clean.

- Remove from the oven and let the cakes cool in the pans for 10 minutes. Then, transfer them to a wire rack to cool completely before frosting.
2. Make the cream cheese frosting:
    - In a large mixing bowl, beat the softened butter and cream cheese until smooth and creamy.
    - Gradually add the powdered sugar, one cup at a time, beating well after each addition.
    - Mix in the vanilla extract until smooth and fluffy. Beat on medium-high speed for 3-4 minutes until light and creamy.
3. Assemble the cake:
    - Once the cakes are completely cooled, level the tops if necessary using a serrated knife.
    - Place one cake layer on a serving plate or cake stand.
    - Spread a layer of cream cheese frosting evenly over the cake layer.
    - Add the next cake layer on top and repeat with more frosting.
    - Add the final cake layer on top.
    - Frost the entire cake with a thin layer of cream cheese frosting to create a crumb coat. Chill the cake in the refrigerator for 30 minutes to set the crumb coat.
    - Finish frosting the cake with the remaining cream cheese frosting, smoothing the sides and top with an offset spatula or bench scraper.
4. Decorate (optional):
    - Optionally, garnish with a sprinkle of ground cinnamon or pumpkin spice on top for decoration.
    - Add edible fall-themed decorations like fondant leaves or flowers for a seasonal touch.
5. Serve and enjoy!
    - Refrigerate the Pumpkin Spice Wedding Cake until ready to serve. Let the cake sit at room temperature for about 30 minutes before serving to allow the frosting to soften slightly.

This Pumpkin Spice Wedding Cake is perfect for celebrating autumn weddings or any special occasion where you want to showcase the cozy flavors of pumpkin and spices. It's moist, flavorful, and topped with creamy cream cheese frosting, making it a delightful treat for your guests!

Neapolitan Wedding Cake

Ingredients:

For the chocolate cake:

- 1 3/4 cups all-purpose flour
- 3/4 cup unsweetened cocoa powder
- 1 1/2 teaspoons baking powder
- 1 1/2 teaspoons baking soda
- 1 teaspoon salt
- 2 cups granulated sugar
- 2 large eggs
- 1 cup buttermilk
- 1/2 cup vegetable oil
- 2 teaspoons vanilla extract
- 1 cup boiling water

For the vanilla cake:

- 1 1/2 cups all-purpose flour
- 1 1/2 teaspoons baking powder
- 1/2 teaspoon baking soda
- 1/2 teaspoon salt
- 1/2 cup unsalted butter, softened
- 1 cup granulated sugar
- 2 large eggs
- 1 cup buttermilk
- 1 teaspoon vanilla extract

For the strawberry cake:

- 1 1/2 cups all-purpose flour
- 1 1/2 teaspoons baking powder
- 1/2 teaspoon baking soda
- 1/2 teaspoon salt
- 1/2 cup unsalted butter, softened
- 1 cup granulweted sugar
- 2 large eggs
- 1/2 cup buttermilk
- 1/2 cup strawberry puree (from fresh or frozen strawberries)

For the frosting:

- 2 cups unsalted butter, softened
- 8 cups powdered sugar, sifted

- 1/2 cup heavy cream
- 2 teaspoons vanilla extract
- 1/2 cup cocoa powder (for chocolate frosting)
- 1/2 cup strawberry puree (for strawberry frosting)

Instructions:

1. Prepare the chocolate cake:
    - Preheat your oven to 350°F (175°C). Grease and flour three 8-inch round cake pans.
    - In a large bowl, sift together the flour, cocoa powder, baking powder, baking soda, and salt.
    - In another large mixing bowl, whisk together the sugar, eggs, buttermilk, vegetable oil, and vanilla extract until smooth.
    - Gradually add the dry ingredients to the wet ingredients, mixing until just combined.
    - Carefully stir in the boiling water until the batter is well combined and smooth.
    - Divide the batter evenly among the prepared cake pans.
    - Bake for 30-35 minutes, or until a toothpick inserted into the center of the cakes comes out clean.
    - Remove from the oven and let the cakes cool in the pans for 10 minutes. Then, transfer them to a wire rack to cool completely.
2. Prepare the vanilla cake:
    - Follow the same steps as for the chocolate cake, using the ingredients listed for the vanilla cake. Divide the batter evenly among three 8-inch round cake pans and bake as directed. Let cool completely.
3. Prepare the strawberry cake:
    - Preheat your oven to 350°F (175°C). Grease and flour three 8-inch round cake pans.
    - In a large bowl, sift together the flour, baking powder, baking soda, and salt.
    - In another large mixing bowl, cream the butter and sugar until light and fluffy.
    - Add the eggs one at a time, mixing well after each addition.
    - Mix in the buttermilk and strawberry puree until well combined.
    - Gradually add the dry ingredients to the wet ingredients, mixing until just combined.
    - Divide the batter evenly among the prepared cake pans.
    - Bake for 25-30 minutes, or until a toothpick inserted into the center of the cakes comes out clean.
    - Remove from the oven and let the cakes cool in the pans for 10 minutes. Then, transfer them to a wire rack to cool completely.
4. Make the frosting:
    - In separate bowls, prepare three different frostings: chocolate, vanilla, and strawberry.
    - For each frosting, in a large mixing bowl, beat the softened butter until smooth and creamy.

- Gradually add the powdered sugar, one cup at a time, beating well after each addition.
- Mix in the heavy cream and vanilla extract until the frosting is smooth and fluffy.
- Divide the frosting into three portions.
- Mix cocoa powder into one portion for chocolate frosting.
- Mix strawberry puree into another portion for strawberry frosting.

5. Assemble the cake:
    - Once the cakes are completely cooled, level the tops if necessary using a serrated knife.
    - Place one chocolate cake layer on a serving plate or cake stand.
    - Spread a layer of chocolate frosting evenly over the cake layer.
    - Add one vanilla cake layer on top of the chocolate frosting, and spread a layer of vanilla frosting evenly over this layer.
    - Add one strawberry cake layer on top of the vanilla frosting, and spread a layer of strawberry frosting evenly over this layer.
    - Repeat with remaining layers, alternating the cake flavors and frostings.
    - Frost the entire cake with a thin layer of frosting to create a crumb coat. Chill the cake in the refrigerator for 30 minutes to set the crumb coat.
    - Finish frosting the cake with the remaining frostings, smoothing the sides and top with an offset spatula or bench scraper.
6. Decorate (optional):
    - Optionally, decorate with chocolate curls, fresh strawberries, or sprinkles to complement the Neapolitan theme.
7. Serve and enjoy!
    - Refrigerate the Neapolitan Wedding Cake until ready to serve. Let the cake sit at room temperature for about 30 minutes before serving to allow the frosting to soften slightly.

This Neapolitan Wedding Cake is a beautiful and delicious celebration of classic flavors, perfect for weddings or any special occasion where you want to impress with both taste and presentation. Each layer brings its own unique flavor, creating a harmonious blend that's sure to delight your guests!

Maple Bacon Wedding Cake

Ingredients:

For the maple bacon cake:

- 3 cups all-purpose flour
- 2 teaspoons baking powder
- 1 teaspoon baking soda
- 1/2 teaspoon salt
- 1 cup unsalted butter, softened
- 1 cup granulated sugar
- 1 cup packed light brown sugar
- 4 large eggs
- 1 cup buttermilk
- 1/2 cup pure maple syrup
- 1 teaspoon vanilla extract
- 1 cup cooked and finely chopped bacon (about 10-12 slices)

For the maple buttercream frosting:

- 1 cup unsalted butter, softened
- 4 cups powdered sugar, sifted
- 1/4 cup pure maple syrup
- 1 teaspoon vanilla extract
- Pinch of salt

For garnish:

- Crispy cooked bacon strips (about 6-8 slices), for decoration

Instructions:

1. Prepare the maple bacon cake:
    - Preheat your oven to 350°F (175°C). Grease and flour three 8-inch round cake pans.
    - In a medium bowl, sift together the flour, baking powder, baking soda, and salt.
    - In a large mixing bowl, cream together the softened butter, granulated sugar, and brown sugar until light and fluffy.
    - Add the eggs one at a time, mixing well after each addition.
    - Mix in the buttermilk, maple syrup, and vanilla extract until well combined.
    - Gradually add the dry ingredients to the wet ingredients, mixing until just combined.
    - Fold in the finely chopped bacon until evenly distributed.
    - Divide the batter evenly among the prepared cake pans.

- Bake for 25-30 minutes, or until a toothpick inserted into the center of the cakes comes out clean.
- Remove from the oven and let the cakes cool in the pans for 10 minutes. Then, transfer them to a wire rack to cool completely.
2. Make the maple buttercream frosting:
    - In a large mixing bowl, beat the softened butter until smooth and creamy.
    - Gradually add the powdered sugar, one cup at a time, beating well after each addition.
    - Mix in the maple syrup, vanilla extract, and a pinch of salt until smooth and fluffy. Adjust consistency with more powdered sugar if needed.
3. Assemble the cake:
    - Once the cakes are completely cooled, level the tops if necessary using a serrated knife.
    - Place one cake layer on a serving plate or cake stand.
    - Spread a layer of maple buttercream frosting evenly over the cake layer.
    - Add the next cake layer on top and repeat with more frosting.
    - Add the final cake layer on top.
    - Frost the entire cake with a thin layer of frosting to create a crumb coat. Chill the cake in the refrigerator for 30 minutes to set the crumb coat.
    - Finish frosting the cake with the remaining maple buttercream frosting, smoothing the sides and top with an offset spatula or bench scraper.
4. Decorate:
    - Garnish the top of the cake with crispy cooked bacon strips for a delicious and decorative touch.
5. Serve and enjoy!
    - Refrigerate the Maple Bacon Wedding Cake until ready to serve. Let the cake sit at room temperature for about 30 minutes before serving to allow the frosting to soften slightly.

This Maple Bacon Wedding Cake is a unique and indulgent choice, perfect for couples looking to add a twist to their wedding dessert. The combination of maple syrup-infused cake layers, savory bacon bits, and sweet maple buttercream frosting creates a memorable and delicious cake that's sure to be a hit with your guests!

S'mores Wedding Cake

Ingredients:

For the chocolate cake:

- 2 cups all-purpose flour
- 1 cup unsweetened cocoa powder
- 2 teaspoons baking powder
- 1 1/2 teaspoons baking soda
- 1 teaspoon salt
- 2 cups granulated sugar
- 1 cup vegetable oil
- 4 large eggs
- 1 cup buttermilk
- 1 cup hot water
- 2 teaspoons vanilla extract

For the graham cracker crust:

- 2 cups graham cracker crumbs
- 1/2 cup unsalted butter, melted
- 1/4 cup granulated sugar

For the marshmallow frosting:

- 4 large egg whites
- 1 cup granulated sugar
- 1/4 teaspoon cream of tartar
- 1 teaspoon vanilla extract

For the chocolate ganache:

- 1 cup heavy cream
- 8 ounces semi-sweet chocolate, chopped
- 1 teaspoon vanilla extract

For decoration:

- Mini marshmallows, lightly toasted
- Additional graham cracker crumbs

Instructions:

1. Prepare the chocolate cake:

- Preheat your oven to 350°F (175°C). Grease and flour three 8-inch round cake pans.
- In a large bowl, sift together the flour, cocoa powder, baking powder, baking soda, and salt.
- In another large mixing bowl, whisk together the sugar, vegetable oil, eggs, buttermilk, and vanilla extract until well combined.
- Gradually add the dry ingredients to the wet ingredients, mixing until smooth.
- Carefully add the hot water to the batter, mixing until well combined and smooth.
- Divide the batter evenly among the prepared cake pans.
- Bake for 25-30 minutes, or until a toothpick inserted into the center of the cakes comes out clean.
- Remove from the oven and let the cakes cool in the pans for 10 minutes. Then, transfer them to a wire rack to cool completely.

2. Make the graham cracker crust:
   - In a medium bowl, combine the graham cracker crumbs, melted butter, and sugar until evenly moistened.
   - Press the mixture into the bottom of a 9-inch springform pan or cake ring lined with parchment paper. Press firmly to create a compact crust.
   - Chill the crust in the refrigerator while preparing the other components.

3. Make the marshmallow frosting:
   - In a heatproof bowl, combine the egg whites, sugar, and cream of tartar.
   - Place the bowl over a pot of simmering water (double boiler method) and whisk constantly until the sugar is dissolved and the mixture reaches 160°F (71°C) on a candy thermometer.
   - Remove from heat and transfer the mixture to a stand mixer fitted with a whisk attachment (or use a hand mixer).
   - Beat on high speed until stiff peaks form and the mixture has cooled to room temperature, about 7-10 minutes.
   - Mix in the vanilla extract until well combined.

4. Make the chocolate ganache:
   - In a small saucepan, heat the heavy cream until it just begins to simmer.
   - Remove from heat and pour over the chopped chocolate in a heatproof bowl.
   - Let it sit for 1-2 minutes, then stir gently until smooth and creamy.
   - Stir in the vanilla extract until well combined. Let the ganache cool slightly to thicken.

5. Assemble the cake:
   - Place one chocolate cake layer on a serving plate or cake stand.
   - Spread a layer of marshmallow frosting over the cake layer.
   - Carefully place the graham cracker crust layer on top of the frosting, pressing gently to adhere.
   - Repeat with another layer of cake, marshmallow frosting, and graham cracker crust.
   - Add the final cake layer on top.

- Frost the entire cake with a thin layer of marshmallow frosting to create a crumb coat. Chill the cake in the refrigerator for 30 minutes to set the crumb coat.
- Finish frosting the cake with the remaining marshmallow frosting, smoothing the sides and top with an offset spatula or bench scraper.
6. Decorate:
    - Drizzle the top of the cake with the chocolate ganache, allowing it to drip down the sides.
    - Sprinkle toasted mini marshmallows and graham cracker crumbs over the top for decoration.
7. Serve and enjoy!
    - Refrigerate the S'mores Wedding Cake until ready to serve. Let the cake sit at room temperature for about 30 minutes before serving to allow the frosting to soften slightly.

This S'mores Wedding Cake is a perfect choice for couples who love the classic campfire treat. It combines rich chocolate cake layers, sweet marshmallow frosting, crunchy graham cracker crust, and decadent chocolate ganache, creating a dessert that's sure to wow your guests and make your wedding celebration even more memorable!

Strawberry Champagne Wedding Cake

Ingredients:

For the champagne cake:

- 2 cups cake flour
- 2 teaspoons baking powder
- 1/2 teaspoon baking soda
- 1/2 teaspoon salt
- 1/2 cup unsalted butter, softened
- 1 1/4 cups granulated sugar
- 3 large egg whites
- 1 teaspoon vanilla extract
- 3/4 cup champagne or sparkling wine (room temperature)
- 1/4 cup buttermilk

For the strawberry filling:

- 2 cups fresh strawberries, chopped
- 1/4 cup granulated sugar
- 2 tablespoons champagne or sparkling wine

For the champagne buttercream frosting:

- 1 cup unsalted butter, softened
- 4 cups powdered sugar, sifted
- 1/4 cup champagne or sparkling wine
- 1 teaspoon vanilla extract
- Pink food coloring (optional)

For decoration:

- Fresh strawberries, whole or sliced
- Edible gold leaf or sprinkles (optional)

Instructions:

1. Prepare the champagne cake:
    - Preheat your oven to 350°F (175°C). Grease and flour three 8-inch round cake pans.
    - In a medium bowl, sift together the cake flour, baking powder, baking soda, and salt.
    - In a large mixing bowl, cream together the softened butter and granulated sugar until light and fluffy.
    - Add the egg whites one at a time, mixing well after each addition.

- Mix in the vanilla extract.
- Combine the champagne (or sparkling wine) and buttermilk in a measuring cup.
- Gradually add the dry ingredients to the creamed mixture, alternating with the champagne/buttermilk mixture, beginning and ending with the dry ingredients. Mix until just combined.
- Divide the batter evenly among the prepared cake pans.
- Bake for 20-25 minutes, or until a toothpick inserted into the center of the cakes comes out clean.
- Remove from the oven and let the cakes cool in the pans for 10 minutes. Then, transfer them to a wire rack to cool completely.

2. Make the strawberry filling:
    - In a saucepan, combine the chopped strawberries, granulated sugar, and champagne (or sparkling wine).
    - Cook over medium heat, stirring occasionally, until the strawberries break down and the mixture thickens (about 10-15 minutes).
    - Remove from heat and let cool completely before using.

3. Make the champagne buttercream frosting:
    - In a large mixing bowl, beat the softened butter until smooth and creamy.
    - Gradually add the powdered sugar, one cup at a time, beating well after each addition.
    - Mix in the champagne (or sparkling wine) and vanilla extract until smooth and fluffy.
    - If desired, add a few drops of pink food coloring to achieve a light pink color.

4. Assemble the cake:
    - Once the cakes are completely cooled, level the tops if necessary using a serrated knife.
    - Place one champagne cake layer on a serving plate or cake stand.
    - Spread a layer of champagne buttercream frosting evenly over the cake layer.
    - Spread a layer of strawberry filling over the frosting.
    - Add the next cake layer on top and repeat with more frosting and strawberry filling.
    - Add the final cake layer on top.
    - Frost the entire cake with a thin layer of champagne buttercream frosting to create a crumb coat. Chill the cake in the refrigerator for 30 minutes to set the crumb coat.
    - Finish frosting the cake with the remaining champagne buttercream frosting, smoothing the sides and top with an offset spatula or bench scraper.

5. Decorate:
    - Garnish the top of the cake with fresh strawberries, either whole or sliced.
    - Optionally, decorate with edible gold leaf or sprinkles for an extra touch of elegance.

6. Serve and enjoy!

- Refrigerate the Strawberry Champagne Wedding Cake until ready to serve. Let the cake sit at room temperature for about 30 minutes before serving to allow the frosting to soften slightly.

This Strawberry Champagne Wedding Cake is a delightful combination of light and fluffy champagne-infused cake layers, sweet strawberry filling, and creamy champagne buttercream frosting. It's perfect for celebrating a wedding with its romantic flavors and elegant presentation!

Chai Latte Wedding Cake

Ingredients:

For the chai cake:

- 2 cups cake flour
- 2 teaspoons baking powder
- 1/2 teaspoon baking soda
- 1/2 teaspoon salt
- 2 teaspoons ground cinnamon
- 1 teaspoon ground ginger
- 1/2 teaspoon ground cardamom
- 1/4 teaspoon ground cloves
- 1/4 teaspoon ground nutmeg
- 1 cup unsalted butter, softened
- 1 1/4 cups granulated sugar
- 3 large eggs
- 1 teaspoon vanilla extract
- 1 cup buttermilk, room temperature
- 1/4 cup brewed strong chai tea, cooled

For the latte frosting:

- 1 cup unsalted butter, softened
- 4 cups powdered sugar, sifted
- 2-3 tablespoons brewed strong chai tea, cooled
- 2-3 tablespoons milk or cream
- 1 teaspoon vanilla extract

For decoration (optional):

- Ground cinnamon or chai spice blend
- Edible gold leaf or sprinkles
- Chai tea bags or whole spices for garnish

Instructions:

1. Prepare the chai cake:
    - Preheat your oven to 350°F (175°C). Grease and flour three 8-inch round cake pans.
    - In a medium bowl, sift together the cake flour, baking powder, baking soda, salt, and spices (cinnamon, ginger, cardamom, cloves, nutmeg).
    - In a large mixing bowl, cream together the softened butter and granulated sugar until light and fluffy.
    - Add the eggs one at a time, mixing well after each addition.

- Mix in the vanilla extract.
- Combine the buttermilk and brewed chai tea in a measuring cup.
- Gradually add the dry ingredients to the creamed mixture, alternating with the buttermilk/chai tea mixture, beginning and ending with the dry ingredients. Mix until just combined.
- Divide the batter evenly among the prepared cake pans.
- Bake for 20-25 minutes, or until a toothpick inserted into the center of the cakes comes out clean.
- Remove from the oven and let the cakes cool in the pans for 10 minutes. Then, transfer them to a wire rack to cool completely.

2. Make the latte frosting:
   - In a large mixing bowl, beat the softened butter until smooth and creamy.
   - Gradually add the powdered sugar, one cup at a time, beating well after each addition.
   - Mix in 2-3 tablespoons of brewed chai tea and 2-3 tablespoons of milk or cream, alternating between them, until you achieve a smooth and spreadable consistency.
   - Mix in the vanilla extract until well combined.

3. Assemble the cake:
   - Once the cakes are completely cooled, level the tops if necessary using a serrated knife.
   - Place one chai cake layer on a serving plate or cake stand.
   - Spread a layer of latte frosting evenly over the cake layer.
   - Add the next cake layer on top and repeat with more frosting.
   - Add the final cake layer on top.
   - Frost the entire cake with a thin layer of latte frosting to create a crumb coat. Chill the cake in the refrigerator for 30 minutes to set the crumb coat.
   - Finish frosting the cake with the remaining latte frosting, smoothing the sides and top with an offset spatula or bench scraper.

4. Decorate (optional):
   - Dust the top of the cake with ground cinnamon or a chai spice blend for decoration.
   - Optionally, add edible gold leaf or sprinkles for an elegant touch.
   - Garnish with chai tea bags or whole spices on top for a decorative finish.

5. Serve and enjoy!
   - Refrigerate the Chai Latte Wedding Cake until ready to serve. Let the cake sit at room temperature for about 30 minutes before serving to allow the frosting to soften slightly.

This Chai Latte Wedding Cake offers a sophisticated twist on traditional flavors, combining the warmth of chai spices with the richness of a latte-inspired frosting. It's a perfect choice for couples looking to add a touch of exotic flavor and elegance to their wedding celebration!

Key Lime Wedding Cake

Ingredients:

For the key lime cake:

- 2 cups cake flour
- 1 teaspoon baking powder
- 1/2 teaspoon baking soda
- 1/2 teaspoon salt
- Zest of 2-3 key limes
- 1/2 cup unsalted butter, softened
- 1 1/4 cups granulated sugar
- 3 large eggs
- 1/2 cup buttermilk
- 1/2 cup fresh key lime juice (about 10-12 key limes)
- 1 teaspoon vanilla extract

For the key lime cream cheese frosting:

- 1/2 cup unsalted butter, softened
- 8 ounces cream cheese, softened
- 4 cups powdered sugar, sifted
- Zest of 1-2 key limes
- 2-3 tablespoons fresh key lime juice
- 1 teaspoon vanilla extract

For decoration (optional):

- Fresh key lime slices or zest
- Edible flowers (such as pansies or violets)
- White chocolate curls or shavings

Instructions:

1. Prepare the key lime cake:
    - Preheat your oven to 350°F (175°C). Grease and flour three 8-inch round cake pans.
    - In a medium bowl, sift together the cake flour, baking powder, baking soda, and salt. Stir in the key lime zest.
    - In a large mixing bowl, cream together the softened butter and granulated sugar until light and fluffy.
    - Add the eggs one at a time, mixing well after each addition.
    - Mix in the buttermilk, fresh key lime juice, and vanilla extract until well combined.
    - Gradually add the dry ingredients to the wet ingredients, mixing until just combined.

- Divide the batter evenly among the prepared cake pans.
- Bake for 20-25 minutes, or until a toothpick inserted into the center of the cakes comes out clean.
- Remove from the oven and let the cakes cool in the pans for 10 minutes. Then, transfer them to a wire rack to cool completely.
2. Make the key lime cream cheese frosting:
    - In a large mixing bowl, beat the softened butter and cream cheese until smooth and creamy.
    - Gradually add the powdered sugar, one cup at a time, beating well after each addition.
    - Mix in the key lime zest, fresh key lime juice, and vanilla extract until smooth and fluffy. Adjust consistency with more powdered sugar if needed.
3. Assemble the cake:
    - Once the cakes are completely cooled, level the tops if necessary using a serrated knife.
    - Place one key lime cake layer on a serving plate or cake stand.
    - Spread a layer of key lime cream cheese frosting evenly over the cake layer.
    - Add the next cake layer on top and repeat with more frosting.
    - Add the final cake layer on top.
    - Frost the entire cake with a thin layer of key lime cream cheese frosting to create a crumb coat. Chill the cake in the refrigerator for 30 minutes to set the crumb coat.
    - Finish frosting the cake with the remaining key lime cream cheese frosting, smoothing the sides and top with an offset spatula or bench scraper.
4. Decorate (optional):
    - Garnish the top of the cake with fresh key lime slices or zest for a vibrant touch.
    - Optionally, decorate with edible flowers like pansies or violets for an elegant look.
    - Sprinkle with white chocolate curls or shavings for added texture and decoration.
5. Serve and enjoy!
    - Refrigerate the Key Lime Wedding Cake until ready to serve. Let the cake sit at room temperature for about 30 minutes before serving to allow the frosting to soften slightly.

This Key Lime Wedding Cake is a refreshing and tangy choice, perfect for couples who appreciate citrus flavors and want to add a bright and flavorful dessert to their wedding celebration. It's sure to be a hit with its zesty key lime cake layers and creamy cream cheese frosting!

Honey Lavender Wedding Cake

Ingredients:

For the lavender cake:

- 2 cups cake flour
- 2 teaspoons baking powder
- 1/2 teaspoon baking soda
- 1/2 teaspoon salt
- 2 tablespoons dried culinary lavender, finely ground
- 1/2 cup unsalted butter, softened
- 1 1/4 cups granulated sugar
- 3 large eggs
- 1 teaspoon vanilla extract
- 1 cup buttermilk
- 1/4 cup honey

For the honey lavender buttercream frosting:

- 1 cup unsalted butter, softened
- 4 cups powdered sugar, sifted
- 2-3 tablespoons honey
- 2-3 tablespoons milk or cream
- 1-2 teaspoons dried culinary lavender, finely ground (adjust to taste)
- Purple food coloring (optional)

For decoration:

- Fresh lavender sprigs (for garnish)
- Edible gold leaf or sprinkles (optional)

Instructions:

1. Prepare the lavender cake:
    - Preheat your oven to 350°F (175°C). Grease and flour three 8-inch round cake pans.
    - In a medium bowl, sift together the cake flour, baking powder, baking soda, salt, and finely ground dried lavender.
    - In a large mixing bowl, cream together the softened butter and granulated sugar until light and fluffy.
    - Add the eggs one at a time, mixing well after each addition.
    - Mix in the vanilla extract.
    - Combine the buttermilk and honey in a measuring cup.

- Gradually add the dry ingredients to the creamed mixture, alternating with the buttermilk/honey mixture, beginning and ending with the dry ingredients. Mix until just combined.
- Divide the batter evenly among the prepared cake pans.
- Bake for 20-25 minutes, or until a toothpick inserted into the center of the cakes comes out clean.
- Remove from the oven and let the cakes cool in the pans for 10 minutes. Then, transfer them to a wire rack to cool completely.

2. Make the honey lavender buttercream frosting:
    - In a large mixing bowl, beat the softened butter until smooth and creamy.
    - Gradually add the powdered sugar, one cup at a time, beating well after each addition.
    - Mix in 2-3 tablespoons of honey and 2-3 tablespoons of milk or cream, alternating between them, until you achieve a smooth and spreadable consistency.
    - Mix in the finely ground dried lavender. Adjust the amount to taste and desired strength of lavender flavor.
    - If desired, add a few drops of purple food coloring to achieve a light lavender color.
3. Assemble the cake:
    - Once the cakes are completely cooled, level the tops if necessary using a serrated knife.
    - Place one lavender cake layer on a serving plate or cake stand.
    - Spread a layer of honey lavender buttercream frosting evenly over the cake layer.
    - Add the next cake layer on top and repeat with more frosting.
    - Add the final cake layer on top.
    - Frost the entire cake with a thin layer of honey lavender buttercream frosting to create a crumb coat. Chill the cake in the refrigerator for 30 minutes to set the crumb coat.
    - Finish frosting the cake with the remaining honey lavender buttercream frosting, smoothing the sides and top with an offset spatula or bench scraper.
4. Decorate:
    - Garnish the top of the cake with fresh lavender sprigs for a beautiful and fragrant touch.
    - Optionally, add edible gold leaf or sprinkles for an elegant finish.
5. Serve and enjoy!
    - Refrigerate the Honey Lavender Wedding Cake until ready to serve. Let the cake sit at room temperature for about 30 minutes before serving to allow the frosting to soften slightly.

This Honey Lavender Wedding Cake offers a delicate balance of floral lavender notes and sweet honey, making it a perfect choice for a wedding cake that is both elegant and flavorful. It's sure to impress with its unique flavor profile and beautiful presentation!

Peaches and Cream Wedding Cake

Ingredients:

For the peach cake:

- 2 cups cake flour
- 1 1/2 teaspoons baking powder
- 1/2 teaspoon baking soda
- 1/2 teaspoon salt
- 1/2 cup unsalted butter, softened
- 1 cup granulated sugar
- 2 large eggs
- 1 teaspoon vanilla extract
- 1/2 cup sour cream
- 1/2 cup buttermilk
- 1 cup finely diced ripe peaches (about 2 medium peaches)

For the peach filling:

- 2 cups ripe peaches, peeled and diced
- 1/4 cup granulated sugar
- 1 tablespoon cornstarch
- 1/4 cup water
- 1 tablespoon lemon juice

For the cream cheese frosting:

- 1/2 cup unsalted butter, softened
- 8 ounces cream cheese, softened
- 4 cups powdered sugar, sifted
- 1 teaspoon vanilla extract

For decoration:

- Fresh peach slices
- Edible flowers (optional)
- Peach preserves or syrup for brushing (optional)

Instructions:

1. Prepare the peach cake:
    - Preheat your oven to 350°F (175°C). Grease and flour three 8-inch round cake pans.
    - In a medium bowl, sift together the cake flour, baking powder, baking soda, and salt.
    - In a large mixing bowl, cream together the softened butter and granulated sugar until light and fluffy.

- Add the eggs one at a time, mixing well after each addition.
- Mix in the vanilla extract.
- In a separate bowl, whisk together the sour cream and buttermilk.
- Gradually add the dry ingredients to the creamed mixture, alternating with the sour cream/buttermilk mixture, beginning and ending with the dry ingredients. Mix until just combined.
- Gently fold in the finely diced peaches.
- Divide the batter evenly among the prepared cake pans.
- Bake for 20-25 minutes, or until a toothpick inserted into the center of the cakes comes out clean.
- Remove from the oven and let the cakes cool in the pans for 10 minutes. Then, transfer them to a wire rack to cool completely.

2. Make the peach filling:
   - In a saucepan, combine the diced peaches, granulated sugar, cornstarch, water, and lemon juice.
   - Cook over medium heat, stirring frequently, until the mixture thickens and the peaches are softened (about 5-7 minutes).
   - Remove from heat and let cool completely before using.

3. Make the cream cheese frosting:
   - In a large mixing bowl, beat the softened butter and cream cheese until smooth and creamy.
   - Gradually add the powdered sugar, one cup at a time, beating well after each addition.
   - Mix in the vanilla extract until smooth and fluffy.

4. Assemble the cake:
   - Once the cakes are completely cooled, level the tops if necessary using a serrated knife.
   - Place one peach cake layer on a serving plate or cake stand.
   - Spread a layer of cream cheese frosting evenly over the cake layer.
   - Spoon a layer of peach filling over the frosting.
   - Add the next cake layer on top and repeat with more frosting and peach filling.
   - Add the final cake layer on top.
   - Frost the entire cake with a thin layer of cream cheese frosting to create a crumb coat. Chill the cake in the refrigerator for 30 minutes to set the crumb coat.
   - Finish frosting the cake with the remaining cream cheese frosting, smoothing the sides and top with an offset spatula or bench scraper.

5. Decorate:
   - Garnish the top of the cake with fresh peach slices and edible flowers for a beautiful presentation.
   - Optionally, brush the peach slices on top with peach preserves or syrup for added shine and flavor.

6. Serve and enjoy!

- Refrigerate the Peaches and Cream Wedding Cake until ready to serve. Let the cake sit at room temperature for about 30 minutes before serving to allow the frosting to soften slightly.

This Peaches and Cream Wedding Cake combines the sweetness of ripe peaches with the richness of cream cheese frosting, creating a delicious and visually stunning dessert that's perfect for celebrating a special occasion like a wedding. It's sure to be a hit with its fresh and fruity flavors!

Baileys Irish Cream Wedding Cake

Ingredients:

For the Baileys Irish Cream cake:

- 2 cups cake flour
- 1 1/2 teaspoons baking powder
- 1/2 teaspoon baking soda
- 1/2 teaspoon salt
- 1/2 cup unsalted butter, softened
- 1 1/4 cups granulated sugar
- 3 large eggs
- 1 teaspoon vanilla extract
- 1/2 cup sour cream
- 1/2 cup Baileys Irish Cream liqueur
- 1/4 cup whole milk

For the Baileys Irish Cream buttercream frosting:

- 1 cup unsalted butter, softened
- 4 cups powdered sugar, sifted
- 1/4 cup Baileys Irish Cream liqueur
- 1 teaspoon vanilla extract
- Pinch of salt

For decoration (optional):

- Chocolate shavings or curls
- Edible gold leaf or sprinkles
- Fresh flowers or berries for garnish

Instructions:

1. Prepare the Baileys Irish Cream cake:
    - Preheat your oven to 350°F (175°C). Grease and flour three 8-inch round cake pans.
    - In a medium bowl, sift together the cake flour, baking powder, baking soda, and salt.
    - In a large mixing bowl, cream together the softened butter and granulated sugar until light and fluffy.
    - Add the eggs one at a time, mixing well after each addition.
    - Mix in the vanilla extract.
    - In a separate bowl, whisk together the sour cream, Baileys Irish Cream liqueur, and whole milk.

- Gradually add the dry ingredients to the creamed mixture, alternating with the sour cream/Baileys mixture, beginning and ending with the dry ingredients. Mix until just combined.
- Divide the batter evenly among the prepared cake pans.
- Bake for 20-25 minutes, or until a toothpick inserted into the center of the cakes comes out clean.
- Remove from the oven and let the cakes cool in the pans for 10 minutes. Then, transfer them to a wire rack to cool completely.

2. Make the Baileys Irish Cream buttercream frosting:
   - In a large mixing bowl, beat the softened butter until smooth and creamy.
   - Gradually add the powdered sugar, one cup at a time, beating well after each addition.
   - Mix in the Baileys Irish Cream liqueur, vanilla extract, and a pinch of salt. Beat until smooth and fluffy. Adjust consistency with more powdered sugar if needed.

3. Assemble the cake:
   - Once the cakes are completely cooled, level the tops if necessary using a serrated knife.
   - Place one Baileys Irish Cream cake layer on a serving plate or cake stand.
   - Spread a layer of Baileys Irish Cream buttercream frosting evenly over the cake layer.
   - Add the next cake layer on top and repeat with more frosting.
   - Add the final cake layer on top.
   - Frost the entire cake with a thin layer of Baileys Irish Cream buttercream frosting to create a crumb coat. Chill the cake in the refrigerator for 30 minutes to set the crumb coat.
   - Finish frosting the cake with the remaining Baileys Irish Cream buttercream frosting, smoothing the sides and top with an offset spatula or bench scraper.

4. Decorate (optional):
   - Garnish the top of the cake with chocolate shavings or curls for a luxurious touch.
   - Optionally, add edible gold leaf or sprinkles for an elegant finish.
   - Decorate with fresh flowers or berries for a beautiful and natural garnish.

5. Serve and enjoy!
   - Refrigerate the Baileys Irish Cream Wedding Cake until ready to serve. Let the cake sit at room temperature for about 30 minutes before serving to allow the frosting to soften slightly.

This Baileys Irish Cream Wedding Cake is a decadent and indulgent choice, perfect for couples who appreciate the rich flavors of Irish cream liqueur. It's sure to be a memorable addition to any wedding celebration with its creamy texture and delightful taste!

Rosewater Pistachio Wedding Cake

Ingredients:

For the pistachio cake:

- 1 cup unsalted shelled pistachios
- 2 cups cake flour
- 1 tablespoon baking powder
- 1/2 teaspoon salt
- 1 cup unsalted butter, softened
- 1 1/2 cups granulated sugar
- 4 large eggs
- 1 teaspoon vanilla extract
- 1 cup milk
- 1/2 teaspoon almond extract (optional)

For the rosewater buttercream frosting:

- 1 cup unsalted butter, softened
- 4 cups powdered sugar, sifted
- 2-3 tablespoons rosewater
- 1-2 tablespoons heavy cream or milk
- Pink or rose food coloring (optional)

For decoration:

- Chopped pistachios for garnish
- Edible rose petals (optional)
- Pistachio macarons or whole pistachios for decoration

Instructions:

1. Prepare the pistachio cake:
    - Preheat your oven to 350°F (175°C). Grease and flour three 8-inch round cake pans.
    - In a food processor or blender, pulse the pistachios until finely ground but not paste-like. Set aside.
    - In a medium bowl, whisk together the cake flour, baking powder, and salt. Stir in the ground pistachios.
    - In a large mixing bowl, cream together the softened butter and granulated sugar until light and fluffy.
    - Add the eggs one at a time, mixing well after each addition.
    - Mix in the vanilla extract and almond extract (if using).
    - Gradually add the dry ingredients to the creamed mixture, alternating with the milk, beginning and ending with the dry ingredients. Mix until just combined.

- Divide the batter evenly among the prepared cake pans.
- Bake for 20-25 minutes, or until a toothpick inserted into the center of the cakes comes out clean.
- Remove from the oven and let the cakes cool in the pans for 10 minutes. Then, transfer them to a wire rack to cool completely.
2. Make the rosewater buttercream frosting:
    - In a large mixing bowl, beat the softened butter until smooth and creamy.
    - Gradually add the powdered sugar, one cup at a time, beating well after each addition.
    - Mix in 2-3 tablespoons of rosewater and 1-2 tablespoons of heavy cream or milk, alternating between them, until you achieve a smooth and spreadable consistency.
    - If desired, add a few drops of pink or rose food coloring to achieve a light pink hue.
3. Assemble the cake:
    - Once the cakes are completely cooled, level the tops if necessary using a serrated knife.
    - Place one pistachio cake layer on a serving plate or cake stand.
    - Spread a layer of rosewater buttercream frosting evenly over the cake layer.
    - Add the next cake layer on top and repeat with more frosting.
    - Add the final cake layer on top.
    - Frost the entire cake with a thin layer of rosewater buttercream frosting to create a crumb coat. Chill the cake in the refrigerator for 30 minutes to set the crumb coat.
    - Finish frosting the cake with the remaining rosewater buttercream frosting, smoothing the sides and top with an offset spatula or bench scraper.
4. Decorate:
    - Sprinkle chopped pistachios around the base of the cake and on top for added texture and flavor.
    - Optionally, decorate with edible rose petals for a delicate and elegant touch.
    - Arrange pistachio macarons or whole pistachios on top of the cake for a decorative finish.
5. Serve and enjoy!
    - Refrigerate the Rosewater Pistachio Wedding Cake until ready to serve. Let the cake sit at room temperature for about 30 minutes before serving to allow the frosting to soften slightly.

This Rosewater Pistachio Wedding Cake offers a sophisticated blend of flavors and textures, making it a perfect choice for a wedding celebration. It's sure to impress with its delicate rosewater essence and nutty pistachio undertones!

Almond Joy Wedding Cake

Ingredients:

For the chocolate cake:

- 2 cups all-purpose flour
- 1 1/2 cups granulated sugar
- 3/4 cup unsweetened cocoa powder
- 2 teaspoons baking powder
- 1 1/2 teaspoons baking soda
- 1 teaspoon salt
- 2 large eggs
- 1 cup milk
- 1/2 cup vegetable oil
- 2 teaspoons vanilla extract
- 1 cup boiling water

For the coconut filling:

- 1 can (14 ounces) sweetened condensed milk
- 1 1/2 cups sweetened shredded coconut

For the chocolate ganache:

- 1 cup heavy cream
- 12 ounces semisweet chocolate, finely chopped

For the almond buttercream frosting:

- 1 cup unsalted butter, softened
- 4 cups powdered sugar, sifted
- 1 teaspoon almond extract
- 2-3 tablespoons milk or cream
- 1/2 cup sliced almonds, toasted

Instructions:

1. Prepare the chocolate cake:
    - Preheat your oven to 350°F (175°C). Grease and flour three 8-inch round cake pans.
    - In a large mixing bowl, sift together the flour, sugar, cocoa powder, baking powder, baking soda, and salt.
    - Add the eggs, milk, oil, and vanilla extract to the dry ingredients and mix until well combined.

- Gradually add the boiling water, mixing until the batter is smooth. The batter will be thin.
- Divide the batter evenly among the prepared cake pans.
- Bake for 30-35 minutes, or until a toothpick inserted into the center of the cakes comes out clean.
- Remove from the oven and let the cakes cool in the pans for 10 minutes. Then, transfer them to a wire rack to cool completely.

2. Make the coconut filling:
   - In a medium saucepan, combine the sweetened condensed milk and sweetened shredded coconut.
   - Cook over medium heat, stirring constantly, until the mixture thickens and starts to pull away from the sides of the pan (about 5-7 minutes).
   - Remove from heat and let cool completely before using.

3. Make the chocolate ganache:
   - Place the finely chopped chocolate in a heatproof bowl.
   - In a small saucepan, heat the heavy cream over medium heat until it just begins to simmer (do not boil).
   - Pour the hot cream over the chopped chocolate and let it sit for 1-2 minutes.
   - Gently stir the mixture with a spatula until the chocolate is completely melted and smooth. Let cool to room temperature before using.

4. Make the almond buttercream frosting:
   - In a large mixing bowl, beat the softened butter until smooth and creamy.
   - Gradually add the powdered sugar, one cup at a time, beating well after each addition.
   - Mix in the almond extract.
   - Add milk or cream, 1 tablespoon at a time, until the frosting reaches a smooth and spreadable consistency.

5. Assemble the cake:
   - Once the cakes are completely cooled, level the tops if necessary using a serrated knife.
   - Place one chocolate cake layer on a serving plate or cake stand.
   - Spread a layer of coconut filling evenly over the cake layer.
   - Add the next chocolate cake layer on top and repeat with more coconut filling.
   - Add the final chocolate cake layer on top.
   - Frost the entire cake with almond buttercream frosting, smoothing the sides and top with an offset spatula or bench scraper.

6. Decorate:
   - Pour the cooled chocolate ganache over the top of the cake, allowing it to drip down the sides.
   - Sprinkle toasted sliced almonds over the top of the cake for added crunch and flavor.
   - Optionally, decorate with additional shredded coconut or chocolate curls for an extra touch.

7. Serve and enjoy!

- Refrigerate the Almond Joy Wedding Cake until ready to serve. Let the cake sit at room temperature for about 30 minutes before serving to allow the frosting and ganache to soften slightly.

This Almond Joy Wedding Cake is sure to be a crowd-pleaser with its layers of moist chocolate cake, creamy coconut filling, rich chocolate ganache, and almond-flavored buttercream frosting. It's a delightful treat that brings together all the flavors of the classic candy bar into a stunning wedding dessert!

Mocha Hazelnut Wedding Cake

Ingredients:

For the hazelnut cake:

- 1 cup unsalted butter, softened
- 1 1/2 cups granulated sugar
- 4 large eggs
- 2 teaspoons vanilla extract
- 2 cups all-purpose flour
- 2 teaspoons baking powder
- 1/2 teaspoon baking soda
- 1/2 teaspoon salt
- 1 cup buttermilk
- 1 cup finely ground hazelnuts (toasted and skins removed)

For the mocha buttercream frosting:

- 1 cup unsalted butter, softened
- 4 cups powdered sugar, sifted
- 1/4 cup unsweetened cocoa powder
- 2-3 tablespoons instant espresso powder (adjust to taste)
- 2-3 tablespoons milk or cream
- 1 teaspoon vanilla extract

For the chocolate ganache:

- 1 cup heavy cream
- 12 ounces semisweet chocolate, finely chopped
- 1 tablespoon instant espresso powder

For decoration:

- Whole hazelnuts, toasted and chopped for garnish
- Chocolate curls or shavings

Instructions:

1. Prepare the hazelnut cake:
    - Preheat your oven to 350°F (175°C). Grease and flour three 8-inch round cake pans.
    - In a large mixing bowl, cream together the softened butter and granulated sugar until light and fluffy.
    - Add the eggs one at a time, mixing well after each addition.
    - Mix in the vanilla extract.

- In a separate bowl, whisk together the flour, baking powder, baking soda, and salt.
- Gradually add the dry ingredients to the creamed mixture, alternating with the buttermilk, beginning and ending with the dry ingredients. Mix until just combined.
- Fold in the finely ground hazelnuts until evenly distributed.
- Divide the batter evenly among the prepared cake pans.
- Bake for 25-30 minutes, or until a toothpick inserted into the center of the cakes comes out clean.
- Remove from the oven and let the cakes cool in the pans for 10 minutes. Then, transfer them to a wire rack to cool completely.

2. Make the mocha buttercream frosting:
   - In a large mixing bowl, beat the softened butter until smooth and creamy.
   - Gradually add the powdered sugar, one cup at a time, beating well after each addition.
   - Mix in the cocoa powder and instant espresso powder.
   - Add milk or cream, 1 tablespoon at a time, until the frosting reaches a smooth and spreadable consistency.
   - Mix in the vanilla extract until well combined.

3. Make the chocolate ganache:
   - Place the finely chopped chocolate and instant espresso powder in a heatproof bowl.
   - In a small saucepan, heat the heavy cream over medium heat until it just begins to simmer (do not boil).
   - Pour the hot cream over the chopped chocolate and let it sit for 1-2 minutes.
   - Gently stir the mixture with a spatula until the chocolate is completely melted and smooth. Let cool to room temperature before using.

4. Assemble the cake:
   - Once the cakes are completely cooled, level the tops if necessary using a serrated knife.
   - Place one hazelnut cake layer on a serving plate or cake stand.
   - Spread a layer of mocha buttercream frosting evenly over the cake layer.
   - Drizzle a layer of chocolate ganache over the frosting.
   - Add the next hazelnut cake layer on top and repeat with more frosting and ganache.
   - Add the final hazelnut cake layer on top.
   - Frost the entire cake with mocha buttercream frosting, smoothing the sides and top with an offset spatula or bench scraper.

5. Decorate:
   - Garnish the top of the cake with toasted and chopped whole hazelnuts for added crunch and flavor.
   - Optionally, decorate with chocolate curls or shavings for an elegant finish.

6. Serve and enjoy!

- Refrigerate the Mocha Hazelnut Wedding Cake until ready to serve. Let the cake sit at room temperature for about 30 minutes before serving to allow the frosting and ganache to soften slightly.

This Mocha Hazelnut Wedding Cake is a perfect blend of rich flavors and textures, making it a delightful choice for a wedding celebration. It combines the nutty aroma of hazelnuts with the richness of chocolate and the boldness of espresso, ensuring a memorable dessert for your special day!

Blueberry Lemon Wedding Cake

Ingredients:

For the blueberry lemon cake:

- 2 1/2 cups cake flour
- 2 teaspoons baking powder
- 1/2 teaspoon baking soda
- 1/2 teaspoon salt
- 1 cup unsalted butter, softened
- 1 1/2 cups granulated sugar
- 4 large eggs
- 1 teaspoon vanilla extract
- Zest of 2 lemons
- 1/4 cup fresh lemon juice
- 1 cup buttermilk
- 1 1/2 cups fresh blueberries (tossed in 1 tablespoon flour)

For the lemon cream cheese frosting:

- 1/2 cup unsalted butter, softened
- 8 ounces cream cheese, softened
- 4 cups powdered sugar, sifted
- Zest of 1 lemon
- 2 tablespoons fresh lemon juice
- 1 teaspoon vanilla extract

For decoration:

- Fresh blueberries
- Lemon slices
- Edible flowers (optional)

Instructions:

1. Prepare the blueberry lemon cake:
    - Preheat your oven to 350°F (175°C). Grease and flour three 8-inch round cake pans.
    - In a medium bowl, sift together the cake flour, baking powder, baking soda, and salt.
    - In a large mixing bowl, cream together the softened butter and granulated sugar until light and fluffy.
    - Add the eggs one at a time, mixing well after each addition.
    - Mix in the vanilla extract, lemon zest, and fresh lemon juice.

- Gradually add the dry ingredients to the creamed mixture, alternating with the buttermilk, beginning and ending with the dry ingredients. Mix until just combined.
- Gently fold in the flour-coated blueberries.
- Divide the batter evenly among the prepared cake pans.
- Bake for 25-30 minutes, or until a toothpick inserted into the center of the cakes comes out clean.
- Remove from the oven and let the cakes cool in the pans for 10 minutes. Then, transfer them to a wire rack to cool completely.

2. Make the lemon cream cheese frosting:
    - In a large mixing bowl, beat the softened butter and cream cheese until smooth and creamy.
    - Gradually add the powdered sugar, one cup at a time, beating well after each addition.
    - Mix in the lemon zest, fresh lemon juice, and vanilla extract until smooth and fluffy.
3. Assemble the cake:
    - Once the cakes are completely cooled, level the tops if necessary using a serrated knife.
    - Place one blueberry lemon cake layer on a serving plate or cake stand.
    - Spread a layer of lemon cream cheese frosting evenly over the cake layer.
    - Add the next cake layer on top and repeat with more frosting.
    - Add the final cake layer on top.
    - Frost the entire cake with the lemon cream cheese frosting, smoothing the sides and top with an offset spatula or bench scraper.
4. Decorate:
    - Garnish the top of the cake with fresh blueberries, lemon slices, and edible flowers for a beautiful and elegant presentation.
5. Serve and enjoy!
    - Refrigerate the Blueberry Lemon Wedding Cake until ready to serve. Let the cake sit at room temperature for about 30 minutes before serving to allow the frosting to soften slightly.

This Blueberry Lemon Wedding Cake is sure to impress with its burst of fruity flavors and creamy frosting, making it a perfect choice for celebrating your special day with a refreshing and delightful dessert!

Earl Grey Lemon Wedding Cake

Ingredients:

For the Earl Grey lemon cake:

- 1 cup whole milk
- 4 Earl Grey tea bags (or 3 tablespoons loose Earl Grey tea)
- 2 1/2 cups cake flour
- 2 1/2 teaspoons baking powder
- 1/2 teaspoon baking soda
- 1/2 teaspoon salt
- 1 cup unsalted butter, softened
- 1 3/4 cups granulated sugar
- 4 large eggs
- 1 teaspoon vanilla extract
- Zest of 2 lemons
- 1/4 cup fresh lemon juice

For the Earl Grey syrup:

- 1/2 cup water
- 1/2 cup granulated sugar
- 2 Earl Grey tea bags (or 1 1/2 tablespoons loose Earl Grey tea)

For the lemon buttercream frosting:

- 1 cup unsalted butter, softened
- 4 cups powdered sugar, sifted
- Zest of 1 lemon
- 2 tablespoons fresh lemon juice
- 1 teaspoon vanilla extract
- Pinch of salt

For decoration:

- Lemon slices
- Edible flowers (optional)

Instructions:

1. Prepare the Earl Grey lemon cake:
    - In a small saucepan, heat the whole milk until just simmering. Remove from heat and add the Earl Grey tea bags (or loose tea). Steep for 15-20 minutes, then strain and discard the tea bags (or tea leaves). Allow the milk to cool to room temperature.

- Preheat your oven to 350°F (175°C). Grease and flour three 8-inch round cake pans.
- In a medium bowl, sift together the cake flour, baking powder, baking soda, and salt.
- In a large mixing bowl, cream together the softened butter and granulated sugar until light and fluffy.
- Add the eggs one at a time, mixing well after each addition.
- Mix in the vanilla extract, lemon zest, and fresh lemon juice.
- Gradually add the dry ingredients to the creamed mixture, alternating with the Earl Grey-infused milk, beginning and ending with the dry ingredients. Mix until just combined.
- Divide the batter evenly among the prepared cake pans.
- Bake for 25-30 minutes, or until a toothpick inserted into the center of the cakes comes out clean.
- Remove from the oven and let the cakes cool in the pans for 10 minutes. Then, transfer them to a wire rack to cool completely.

2. Make the Earl Grey syrup:
    - In a small saucepan, combine the water and granulated sugar. Bring to a simmer over medium heat, stirring until the sugar dissolves.
    - Remove from heat and add the Earl Grey tea bags (or loose tea). Steep for 10-15 minutes.
    - Remove the tea bags (or strain out the loose tea) and let the syrup cool to room temperature.
3. Make the lemon buttercream frosting:
    - In a large mixing bowl, beat the softened butter until smooth and creamy.
    - Gradually add the powdered sugar, one cup at a time, beating well after each addition.
    - Mix in the lemon zest, fresh lemon juice, vanilla extract, and a pinch of salt until smooth and fluffy.
4. Assemble the cake:
    - Once the cakes are completely cooled, level the tops if necessary using a serrated knife.
    - Place one Earl Grey lemon cake layer on a serving plate or cake stand.
    - Brush a layer of Earl Grey syrup evenly over the cake layer.
    - Spread a layer of lemon buttercream frosting evenly over the cake layer.
    - Repeat with the remaining cake layers, brushing each with Earl Grey syrup and frosting with lemon buttercream.
    - Frost the entire cake with the lemon buttercream frosting, smoothing the sides and top with an offset spatula or bench scraper.
5. Decorate:
    - Garnish the top of the cake with lemon slices and edible flowers for a fresh and elegant presentation.
6. Serve and enjoy!

- Refrigerate the Earl Grey Lemon Wedding Cake until ready to serve. Let the cake sit at room temperature for about 30 minutes before serving to allow the frosting to soften slightly.

This Earl Grey Lemon Wedding Cake offers a unique and sophisticated flavor combination that is sure to be a hit at any wedding celebration. The infusion of Earl Grey tea adds a subtle floral note, complementing the bright zestiness of lemon in a beautifully balanced dessert.

Banana Nut Wedding Cake

Ingredients:

For the banana nut cake:

- 3 cups all-purpose flour
- 2 teaspoons baking powder
- 1 teaspoon baking soda
- 1/2 teaspoon salt
- 1 cup unsalted butter, softened
- 2 cups granulated sugar
- 4 large eggs
- 2 teaspoons vanilla extract
- 1 cup sour cream
- 1 1/2 cups mashed ripe bananas (about 3-4 bananas)
- 1 cup chopped walnuts or pecans

For the cream cheese frosting:

- 1 cup unsalted butter, softened
- 16 ounces cream cheese, softened
- 6 cups powdered sugar, sifted
- 2 teaspoons vanilla extract

For decoration:

- Additional chopped nuts for garnish
- Banana slices (optional)
- Edible flowers (optional)

Instructions:

1. Prepare the banana nut cake:
    - Preheat your oven to 350°F (175°C). Grease and flour three 8-inch round cake pans.
    - In a medium bowl, sift together the flour, baking powder, baking soda, and salt.
    - In a large mixing bowl, cream together the softened butter and granulated sugar until light and fluffy.
    - Add the eggs one at a time, mixing well after each addition.
    - Mix in the vanilla extract.
    - Combine the sour cream and mashed bananas in a separate bowl.
    - Gradually add the dry ingredients to the creamed mixture, alternating with the banana-sour cream mixture, beginning and ending with the dry ingredients. Mix until just combined.
    - Fold in the chopped nuts until evenly distributed.

- Divide the batter evenly among the prepared cake pans.
- Bake for 25-30 minutes, or until a toothpick inserted into the center of the cakes comes out clean.
- Remove from the oven and let the cakes cool in the pans for 10 minutes. Then, transfer them to a wire rack to cool completely.

2. Make the cream cheese frosting:
   - In a large mixing bowl, beat the softened butter and cream cheese until smooth and creamy.
   - Gradually add the powdered sugar, one cup at a time, beating well after each addition.
   - Mix in the vanilla extract until smooth and fluffy.
3. Assemble the cake:
   - Once the cakes are completely cooled, level the tops if necessary using a serrated knife.
   - Place one banana nut cake layer on a serving plate or cake stand.
   - Spread a layer of cream cheese frosting evenly over the cake layer.
   - Add the next cake layer on top and repeat with more frosting.
   - Add the final cake layer on top.
   - Frost the entire cake with the cream cheese frosting, smoothing the sides and top with an offset spatula or bench scraper.
4. Decorate:
   - Sprinkle chopped nuts over the top of the cake for added texture and flavor.
   - Optionally, garnish with banana slices and edible flowers for an elegant touch.
5. Serve and enjoy!
   - Refrigerate the Banana Nut Wedding Cake until ready to serve. Let the cake sit at room temperature for about 30 minutes before serving to allow the frosting to soften slightly.

This Banana Nut Wedding Cake offers a comforting and flavorful twist on traditional wedding cakes, making it a memorable and delicious choice for celebrating your special day!

Cherry Almond Wedding Cake

Ingredients:

For the cake:

- 2 cups all-purpose flour
- 1 teaspoon baking powder
- 1/2 teaspoon baking soda
- 1/2 teaspoon salt
- 1 cup unsalted butter, softened
- 1 1/2 cups granulated sugar
- 4 large eggs
- 1 teaspoon almond extract
- 1 cup sour cream
- 1/2 cup chopped almonds
- 1 cup maraschino cherries, drained and chopped

For the frosting:

- 1 cup unsalted butter, softened
- 4 cups powdered sugar
- 1/4 cup milk
- 1 teaspoon almond extract
- Additional chopped almonds and maraschino cherries for decorating

Instructions:

1. Preheat your oven to 350°F (175°C). Grease and flour three 8-inch round cake pans.
2. Prepare the cake batter:
    - In a medium bowl, whisk together flour, baking powder, baking soda, and salt.
    - In a separate large bowl, beat butter and sugar together until light and fluffy.
    - Beat in eggs, one at a time, then add almond extract.
    - Gradually add flour mixture alternately with sour cream, beating well after each addition.
    - Fold in chopped almonds and chopped cherries.
3. Bake the cakes:
    - Divide batter evenly among the prepared pans.
    - Bake in preheated oven for 25-30 minutes, or until a toothpick inserted into the center comes out clean.
    - Allow cakes to cool in pans for 10 minutes, then remove from pans and cool completely on wire racks.
4. Make the frosting:
    - In a large bowl, beat butter until creamy.

- Gradually beat in powdered sugar, alternating with milk and almond extract, until frosting reaches spreading consistency.
5. Assemble the cake:
    - Place one cake layer on a serving plate; spread with a layer of frosting.
    - Repeat with remaining layers, stacking the cake.
    - Frost the top and sides of the cake with the remaining frosting.
6. Decorate the cake:
    - Garnish with additional chopped almonds and whole or halved maraschino cherries.
7. Chill the cake until ready to serve. Enjoy your delicious Cherry Almond Wedding Cake!

This cake combines the nutty flavor of almonds with the sweetness of cherries, making it a perfect choice for a wedding or any special occasion!

Salted Caramel Wedding Cake

Ingredients:

For the cake:

- 3 cups all-purpose flour
- 2 teaspoons baking powder
- 1/2 teaspoon baking soda
- 1/2 teaspoon salt
- 1 cup unsalted butter, softened
- 2 cups granulated sugar
- 4 large eggs
- 1 tablespoon vanilla extract
- 1 cup buttermilk
- 1/2 cup salted caramel sauce (plus extra for drizzling)
- 1 cup chopped pecans or walnuts (optional)

For the salted caramel sauce:

- 1 cup granulated sugar
- 6 tablespoons unsalted butter, cut into pieces
- 1/2 cup heavy cream
- 1 teaspoon sea salt

For the frosting:

- 1 cup unsalted butter, softened
- 4 cups powdered sugar
- 1/2 cup salted caramel sauce
- 1-2 tablespoons heavy cream, if needed
- Sea salt, for sprinkling

Instructions:

1. Make the salted caramel sauce:
    - In a heavy-bottomed saucepan, heat granulated sugar over medium heat, stirring constantly with a heat-resistant rubber spatula or wooden spoon.
    - Sugar will form clumps and eventually melt into a thick brown, amber-colored liquid as you continue to stir. Be careful not to burn.
    - Once sugar is completely melted, immediately add the butter. Be careful in this step as the caramel will bubble rapidly when the butter is added.
    - Stir the butter into the caramel until it is completely melted, about 2-3 minutes.
    - Very slowly, drizzle in the heavy cream while stirring. Since the heavy cream is colder than the caramel, the mixture will rapidly bubble and/or splatter when added. Allow the mixture to boil for 1 minute.

Passion Fruit Mango Wedding Cake

Ingredients:

For the cake:

- 3 cups all-purpose flour
- 2 teaspoons baking powder
- 1 teaspoon baking soda
- 1/2 teaspoon salt
- 1 cup unsalted butter, softened
- 2 cups granulated sugar
- 4 large eggs
- 1 teaspoon vanilla extract
- 1 cup buttermilk
- 1/2 cup mango puree (from fresh mangoes)
- Zest of 1 lime
- 1/2 cup passion fruit pulp (fresh or canned)

For the passion fruit mango curd filling:

- 1 cup passion fruit pulp (fresh or canned)
- 1 cup mango puree
- 1/2 cup granulated sugar
- 4 large egg yolks
- 1/4 cup unsalted butter, cut into small pieces

For the frosting:

- 1 1/2 cups unsalted butter, softened
- 6 cups powdered sugar
- 1/2 cup mango puree
- Zest of 1 lime
- Yellow food coloring (optional, for desired color)
- Fresh mango slices, passion fruit seeds, and lime zest for garnish

Instructions:

1. Make the cake:
    - Preheat your oven to 350°F (175°C). Grease and flour three 8-inch round cake pans.
    - In a medium bowl, whisk together the flour, baking powder, baking soda, and salt.
    - In a large bowl, cream together the butter and sugar until light and fluffy.
    - Add eggs one at a time, beating well after each addition. Stir in the vanilla extract.

- Combine the buttermilk, mango puree, lime zest, and passion fruit pulp in another bowl.
- Gradually add the dry ingredients to the butter mixture, alternating with the mango-passion fruit mixture, beginning and ending with the dry ingredients. Mix until just combined.
- Divide the batter evenly among the prepared pans and smooth the tops.
- Bake for 25-30 minutes, or until a toothpick inserted into the center comes out clean.
- Allow the cakes to cool in the pans for 10 minutes, then transfer to wire racks to cool completely.

2. Make the passion fruit mango curd filling:
    - In a medium saucepan, combine the passion fruit pulp, mango puree, sugar, and egg yolks.
    - Cook over medium heat, whisking constantly, until the mixture thickens and coats the back of a spoon (about 8-10 minutes).
    - Remove from heat and stir in the butter until melted and well combined.
    - Transfer the curd to a bowl and press a piece of plastic wrap directly onto the surface to prevent a skin from forming.
    - Chill in the refrigerator until firm.

3. Make the frosting:
    - In a large bowl, beat the softened butter until creamy.
    - Gradually add the powdered sugar, one cup at a time, beating well after each addition.
    - Add the mango puree and lime zest, and beat until light and fluffy. Add yellow food coloring if desired for a more vibrant color.

4. Assemble the cake:
    - Place one cake layer on a serving plate or cake stand.
    - Spread a layer of passion fruit mango curd filling over the cake layer.
    - Top with another cake layer and repeat the filling process.
    - Place the final cake layer on top.

5. Frost the cake:
    - Apply a crumb coat of frosting to the entire cake. Chill for 30 minutes in the refrigerator.
    - Frost the entire cake with the remaining frosting, smoothing the sides and top.

6. Decorate the cake:
    - Garnish the top of the cake with fresh mango slices, passion fruit seeds, and lime zest for a tropical touch.
    - Refrigerate the cake until ready to serve.

7. Serve and enjoy!

This Passion Fruit Mango Wedding Cake will surely impress with its bright flavors and elegant presentation, perfect for celebrating a special day!

Cinnamon Roll Wedding Cake

Ingredients:

For the cake layers:

- 3 cups all-purpose flour
- 2 teaspoons baking powder
- 1/2 teaspoon baking soda
- 1/2 teaspoon salt
- 1 cup unsalted butter, softened
- 1 1/2 cups granulated sugar
- 4 large eggs
- 1 tablespoon vanilla extract
- 1 cup buttermilk

For the cinnamon swirl:

- 1/2 cup unsalted butter, melted
- 1 cup brown sugar, packed
- 2 tablespoons ground cinnamon

For the cream cheese frosting:

- 1 cup unsalted butter, softened
- 16 oz cream cheese, softened
- 6 cups powdered sugar
- 2 teaspoons vanilla extract

For garnish:

- Cinnamon sugar (mix cinnamon with granulated sugar)
- Cinnamon sticks (optional)
- Edible gold or silver leaf (optional)

Instructions:

1. Make the cake layers:
    - Preheat your oven to 350°F (175°C). Grease and flour three 8-inch round cake pans.
    - In a medium bowl, whisk together the flour, baking powder, baking soda, and salt.
    - In a large bowl, cream together the butter and sugar until light and fluffy.
    - Add eggs one at a time, beating well after each addition. Stir in the vanilla extract.
    - Gradually add the dry ingredients to the butter mixture, alternating with the buttermilk, beginning and ending with the dry ingredients. Mix until just combined.

- Divide the batter evenly among the prepared pans and smooth the tops.
- In a small bowl, mix together the melted butter, brown sugar, and ground cinnamon for the cinnamon swirl.
- Spoon and spread the cinnamon swirl mixture evenly over each cake layer.
- Use a knife or skewer to gently swirl the cinnamon mixture into the cake batter, creating a marbled effect.
- Bake for 25-30 minutes, or until a toothpick inserted into the center comes out clean.
- Allow the cakes to cool in the pans for 10 minutes, then transfer to wire racks to cool completely.

2. Make the cream cheese frosting:
   - In a large bowl, beat the softened butter and cream cheese together until smooth and creamy.
   - Gradually add the powdered sugar, one cup at a time, beating well after each addition.
   - Stir in the vanilla extract until well combined.
3. Assemble the cake:
   - Place one cinnamon swirl cake layer on a serving plate or cake stand.
   - Spread a layer of cream cheese frosting over the cake layer.
   - Repeat with the remaining cake layers and frosting, stacking them on top of each other.
   - Frost the entire cake with the remaining cream cheese frosting, smoothing the sides and top.
4. Decorate the cake:
   - Sprinkle the top of the cake with cinnamon sugar for added sweetness and a cinnamon roll-like finish.
   - Optionally, garnish with cinnamon sticks and edible gold or silver leaf for a touch of elegance.
5. Serve and enjoy!

This Cinnamon Roll Wedding Cake combines the comforting flavors of cinnamon and cream cheese frosting, perfect for a cozy and memorable wedding celebration!

Irish Whiskey Chocolate Wedding Cake

Ingredients:

For the cake:

- 2 cups all-purpose flour
- 1 cup unsweetened cocoa powder
- 1 1/2 teaspoons baking powder
- 1 1/2 teaspoons baking soda
- 1 teaspoon salt
- 2 cups granulated sugar
- 1 cup unsalted butter, softened
- 4 large eggs
- 2 teaspoons vanilla extract
- 1 1/2 cups buttermilk
- 1/2 cup Irish whiskey (such as Jameson)

For the Irish whiskey chocolate ganache:

- 1 cup heavy cream
- 8 oz semisweet chocolate, chopped
- 2 tablespoons unsalted butter, softened
- 2 tablespoons Irish whiskey

For the whiskey buttercream frosting:

- 1 1/2 cups unsalted butter, softened
- 5 cups powdered sugar
- 1/4 cup Irish whiskey
- 1 teaspoon vanilla extract
- Pinch of salt

Instructions:

1. Make the cake:
    - Preheat your oven to 350°F (175°C). Grease and flour three 8-inch round cake pans.
    - In a medium bowl, whisk together the flour, cocoa powder, baking powder, baking soda, and salt.
    - In a large bowl, cream together the butter and sugar until light and fluffy.
    - Add eggs one at a time, beating well after each addition. Stir in the vanilla extract.
    - Gradually add the dry ingredients to the butter mixture, alternating with the buttermilk and Irish whiskey, beginning and ending with the dry ingredients. Mix until just combined.

- Divide the batter evenly among the prepared pans and smooth the tops.
    - Bake for 25-30 minutes, or until a toothpick inserted into the center comes out clean.
    - Allow the cakes to cool in the pans for 10 minutes, then transfer to wire racks to cool completely.
2. Make the Irish whiskey chocolate ganache:
    - In a small saucepan, heat the heavy cream over medium heat until it just begins to simmer.
    - Remove from heat and stir in the chopped chocolate until smooth and melted.
    - Stir in the butter and Irish whiskey until well combined.
    - Allow the ganache to cool and thicken slightly before assembling the cake.
3. Make the whiskey buttercream frosting:
    - In a large bowl, beat the softened butter until creamy.
    - Gradually add the powdered sugar, one cup at a time, beating well after each addition.
    - Stir in the Irish whiskey, vanilla extract, and a pinch of salt. Beat until light and fluffy.
4. Assemble the cake:
    - Place one cake layer on a serving plate or cake stand.
    - Spread a layer of whiskey buttercream frosting over the cake layer.
    - Drizzle a generous amount of Irish whiskey chocolate ganache over the frosting.
    - Repeat with the remaining cake layers, frosting, and ganache, stacking them on top of each other.
5. Frost the cake:
    - Frost the entire cake with the remaining whiskey buttercream frosting, smoothing the sides and top.
6. Decorate the cake:
    - Optionally, drizzle additional Irish whiskey chocolate ganache over the top of the cake for a decorative touch.
    - Garnish with chocolate shavings, curls, or sprinkles for added elegance.
7. Chill the cake until ready to serve to allow the flavors to meld together.

This Irish Whiskey Chocolate Wedding Cake will be a show-stopper at any celebration, combining rich chocolate flavors with a delightful hint of Irish whiskey. Perfect for those who appreciate a touch of sophistication and indulgence!

Cardamom Pear Wedding Cake

Ingredients:

For the cake:

- 3 cups all-purpose flour
- 1 tablespoon baking powder
- 1 teaspoon baking soda
- 1/2 teaspoon salt
- 1 teaspoon ground cardamom
- 1 cup unsalted butter, softened
- 1 1/2 cups granulated sugar
- 4 large eggs
- 2 teaspoons vanilla extract
- 1 cup buttermilk
- 2 cups finely chopped ripe pears (about 2 medium pears)

For the cardamom pear filling:

- 2 cups finely chopped ripe pears (about 2 medium pears)
- 1/4 cup granulated sugar
- 1/2 teaspoon ground cardamom
- 1 tablespoon lemon juice
- 1 tablespoon cornstarch

For the cardamom buttercream frosting:

- 1 1/2 cups unsalted butter, softened
- 6 cups powdered sugar
- 1/2 teaspoon ground cardamom
- 2-3 tablespoons milk or cream
- Sliced pears and edible flowers for garnish (optional)

Instructions:

1. Make the cake:
   - Preheat your oven to 350°F (175°C). Grease and flour three 8-inch round cake pans.
   - In a medium bowl, whisk together the flour, baking powder, baking soda, salt, and ground cardamom.
   - In a large bowl, cream together the butter and sugar until light and fluffy.
   - Add eggs one at a time, beating well after each addition. Stir in the vanilla extract.
   - Gradually add the dry ingredients to the butter mixture, alternating with the buttermilk, beginning and ending with the dry ingredients. Mix until just combined.

- Fold in the finely chopped pears until evenly distributed.
- Divide the batter evenly among the prepared pans and smooth the tops.
- Bake for 25-30 minutes, or until a toothpick inserted into the center comes out clean.
- Allow the cakes to cool in the pans for 10 minutes, then transfer to wire racks to cool completely.

2. Make the cardamom pear filling:
   - In a medium saucepan, combine the finely chopped pears, sugar, ground cardamom, lemon juice, and cornstarch.
   - Cook over medium heat, stirring frequently, until the mixture thickens and the pears are tender (about 5-7 minutes).
   - Remove from heat and let cool completely before using as filling.

3. Make the cardamom buttercream frosting:
   - In a large bowl, beat the softened butter until creamy.
   - Gradually add the powdered sugar, one cup at a time, beating well after each addition.
   - Add ground cardamom and milk or cream, beating until light and fluffy. Adjust consistency with more milk or cream if needed.

4. Assemble the cake:
   - Place one cake layer on a serving plate or cake stand.
   - Spread a layer of cardamom buttercream frosting over the cake layer.
   - Spoon a layer of cooled cardamom pear filling over the frosting.
   - Repeat with the remaining cake layers, spreading frosting and filling between each layer.
   - Frost the entire cake with the remaining cardamom buttercream frosting, smoothing the sides and top.

5. Decorate the cake:
   - Arrange sliced pears and edible flowers on top of the cake for a beautiful and elegant presentation.
   - Optionally, sprinkle a little ground cardamom over the top for extra flavor and decoration.

6. Chill the cake until ready to serve to allow the flavors to meld together.

This Cardamom Pear Wedding Cake will be a delightful and unique addition to your special day, combining the warmth of cardamom with the sweetness of ripe pears. Enjoy!

Pineapple Upside-Down Wedding Cake

Ingredients:

For the pineapple topping:

- 1/2 cup unsalted butter
- 1 cup packed brown sugar
- 1 can (20 oz) pineapple slices in juice, drained (reserve juice)
- Maraschino cherries, drained (optional)

For the cake:

- 2 cups all-purpose flour
- 1 1/2 teaspoons baking powder
- 1/2 teaspoon baking soda
- 1/2 teaspoon salt
- 1/2 cup unsalted butter, softened
- 1 cup granulated sugar
- 2 large eggs
- 1 teaspoon vanilla extract
- 1/2 cup buttermilk
- 1/2 cup reserved pineapple juice (from the canned pineapple)

For the frosting:

- 1 1/2 cups unsalted butter, softened
- 6 cups powdered sugar
- 1 teaspoon vanilla extract
- 2-4 tablespoons milk or cream (as needed for consistency)

Instructions:

1. Prepare the pineapple topping:
    - Preheat your oven to 350°F (175°C). Grease and flour three 8-inch round cake pans.
    - In a small saucepan, melt the butter over medium heat.
    - Stir in the brown sugar until melted and smooth. Pour the mixture evenly into the bottom of each cake pan.
    - Arrange the pineapple slices on top of the brown sugar mixture in a decorative pattern. Place a maraschino cherry in the center of each pineapple slice, if desired.
2. Make the cake batter:
    - In a medium bowl, whisk together the flour, baking powder, baking soda, and salt.
    - In a large bowl, cream together the butter and granulated sugar until light and fluffy.

- Add the eggs one at a time, beating well after each addition. Stir in the vanilla extract.
- Gradually add the dry ingredients to the butter mixture, alternating with the buttermilk and reserved pineapple juice, beginning and ending with the dry ingredients. Mix until just combined.
3. Assemble and bake the cake:
    - Divide the cake batter evenly among the prepared cake pans, spreading it carefully over the pineapple slices.
    - Bake for 25-30 minutes, or until a toothpick inserted into the center of the cakes comes out clean.
    - Remove from the oven and let cool in the pans for 10 minutes.
4. Prepare the frosting:
    - In a large bowl, beat the softened butter until creamy.
    - Gradually add the powdered sugar, one cup at a time, beating well after each addition.
    - Stir in the vanilla extract. Add milk or cream, one tablespoon at a time, until the frosting reaches a spreadable consistency.
5. Assemble the cake:
    - Carefully invert each cake layer onto a serving platter or cake stand, pineapple-side up.
    - Let the cakes cool completely.
6. Frost the cake:
    - Once the cakes are completely cooled, frost the top and sides of the cake with the prepared frosting, smoothing it out evenly.
7. Decorate the cake:
    - Optionally, garnish the top of the cake with additional pineapple slices and maraschino cherries for a festive look.
    - Serve and enjoy this delightful Pineapple Upside-Down Wedding Cake!

This cake will impress with its caramelized pineapple topping and moist, flavorful cake layers, making it a memorable choice for your wedding celebration.

Raspberry Almond Wedding Cake

Ingredients:

For the cake:

- 2 cups all-purpose flour
- 1 cup almond flour (ground almonds)
- 1 tablespoon baking powder
- 1/2 teaspoon baking soda
- 1/2 teaspoon salt
- 1 cup unsalted butter, softened
- 1 1/2 cups granulated sugar
- 4 large eggs
- 1 teaspoon almond extract
- 1 cup sour cream
- 1/2 cup milk
- 1 cup fresh raspberries (lightly mashed)

For the raspberry filling:

- 2 cups fresh raspberries
- 1/4 cup granulated sugar
- 1 tablespoon cornstarch
- 1 tablespoon lemon juice

For the almond buttercream frosting:

- 1 1/2 cups unsalted butter, softened
- 6 cups powdered sugar
- 1 teaspoon almond extract
- 2-4 tablespoons milk or cream (as needed for consistency)
- Sliced almonds and fresh raspberries for garnish

Instructions:

1. Make the cake:
    - Preheat your oven to 350°F (175°C). Grease and flour three 8-inch round cake pans.
    - In a medium bowl, whisk together the all-purpose flour, almond flour, baking powder, baking soda, and salt.
    - In a large bowl, cream together the butter and sugar until light and fluffy.
    - Add eggs one at a time, beating well after each addition. Stir in the almond extract.

- Gradually add the dry ingredients to the butter mixture, alternating with the sour cream and milk, beginning and ending with the dry ingredients. Mix until just combined.
    - Gently fold in the mashed raspberries.
    - Divide the batter evenly among the prepared pans and smooth the tops.
    - Bake for 25-30 minutes, or until a toothpick inserted into the center comes out clean.
    - Allow the cakes to cool in the pans for 10 minutes, then transfer to wire racks to cool completely.
2. Make the raspberry filling:
    - In a saucepan, combine the raspberries, sugar, cornstarch, and lemon juice.
    - Cook over medium heat, stirring constantly, until the mixture thickens and comes to a boil.
    - Reduce heat and simmer for 2-3 minutes until the mixture is glossy and thickened.
    - Remove from heat and let cool completely before using as filling.
3. Make the almond buttercream frosting:
    - In a large bowl, beat the softened butter until creamy.
    - Gradually add the powdered sugar, one cup at a time, beating well after each addition.
    - Stir in the almond extract. Add milk or cream, one tablespoon at a time, until the frosting reaches a smooth and spreadable consistency.
4. Assemble the cake:
    - Place one cake layer on a serving plate or cake stand.
    - Spread a layer of almond buttercream frosting over the cake layer.
    - Spoon a layer of raspberry filling over the frosting, spreading it evenly.
    - Repeat with the remaining cake layers, frosting, and filling.
    - Frost the entire cake with the remaining almond buttercream frosting, smoothing the sides and top.
5. Decorate the cake:
    - Garnish the top of the cake with sliced almonds and fresh raspberries for a beautiful presentation.
    - Optionally, drizzle additional raspberry filling over the top for added flavor and decoration.
6. Chill the cake until ready to serve to allow the flavors to meld together.

This Raspberry Almond Wedding Cake will be a lovely addition to your celebration, combining the nuttiness of almond with the brightness of fresh raspberries for a delicious and elegant dessert. Enjoy!

Creme Brulee Wedding Cake

Ingredients:

For the cake layers:

- 3 cups all-purpose flour
- 2 teaspoons baking powder
- 1/2 teaspoon baking soda
- 1/2 teaspoon salt
- 1 cup unsalted butter, softened
- 2 cups granulated sugar
- 4 large eggs
- 1 tablespoon vanilla extract
- 1 cup buttermilk

For the creme brulee filling:

- 4 cups heavy cream
- 1 cup granulated sugar
- 8 large egg yolks
- 2 teaspoons vanilla extract

For the frosting:

- 1 1/2 cups unsalted butter, softened
- 6 cups powdered sugar
- 1 tablespoon vanilla extract
- 2-4 tablespoons heavy cream (as needed for consistency)

For the caramelized sugar topping:

- 1/2 cup granulated sugar
- Fresh berries and mint leaves for garnish (optional)

Instructions:

1. Make the cake layers:
    - Preheat your oven to 350°F (175°C). Grease and flour three 8-inch round cake pans.
    - In a medium bowl, whisk together the flour, baking powder, baking soda, and salt.
    - In a large bowl, cream together the butter and sugar until light and fluffy.
    - Add eggs one at a time, beating well after each addition. Stir in the vanilla extract.
    - Gradually add the dry ingredients to the butter mixture, alternating with the buttermilk, beginning and ending with the dry ingredients. Mix until just combined.

- Divide the batter evenly among the prepared pans and smooth the tops.
- Bake for 25-30 minutes, or until a toothpick inserted into the center comes out clean.
- Allow the cakes to cool in the pans for 10 minutes, then transfer to wire racks to cool completely.

2. Make the creme brulee filling:
   - Preheat your oven to 325°F (160°C).
   - In a saucepan, heat the heavy cream over medium heat until it just begins to simmer. Remove from heat.
   - In a large bowl, whisk together the sugar, egg yolks, and vanilla extract until well combined.
   - Slowly pour the hot cream into the egg yolk mixture, whisking constantly, until smooth and combined.
   - Strain the mixture through a fine mesh sieve to remove any lumps.
   - Divide the mixture evenly among three 8-inch round cake pans (you can use the same pans used for baking the cakes).
   - Place the cake pans in a larger roasting pan or baking dish. Fill the roasting pan with enough hot water to come halfway up the sides of the cake pans.
   - Bake for 30-35 minutes, or until the custard is set but still slightly jiggly in the center.
   - Remove the pans from the water bath and let the custards cool to room temperature. Then refrigerate for at least 4 hours, or overnight, until fully chilled and set.

3. Make the frosting:
   - In a large bowl, beat the softened butter until creamy.
   - Gradually add the powdered sugar, one cup at a time, beating well after each addition.
   - Stir in the vanilla extract. Add heavy cream, one tablespoon at a time, until the frosting reaches a smooth and spreadable consistency.

4. Assemble the cake:
   - Place one cake layer on a serving plate or cake stand.
   - Spread a layer of frosting over the cake layer.
   - Carefully invert one of the chilled creme brulee custards onto the frosting layer.
   - Repeat with the remaining cake layers and creme brulee custards.
   - Frost the entire cake with the remaining frosting, smoothing the sides and top.

5. Caramelize the sugar topping:
   - Sprinkle a thin, even layer of granulated sugar over the top of the frosted cake.
   - Use a culinary torch to carefully caramelize the sugar until it forms a golden brown crust. Alternatively, you can place the cake under a broiler for a few minutes, watching closely to prevent burning.

6. Decorate the cake:
   - Garnish with fresh berries and mint leaves for a fresh and elegant presentation.

7. Chill the cake until ready to serve, and enjoy this decadent Creme Brulee Wedding Cake with its creamy custard filling and caramelized sugar topping, reminiscent of the classic dessert.

This cake is sure to be a show-stopper at your wedding, combining the sophistication of creme brulee with the celebration of cake!

Coconut Lime Wedding Cake

Ingredients:

For the cake:

- 3 cups cake flour
- 1 tablespoon baking powder
- 1/2 teaspoon baking soda
- 1/2 teaspoon salt
- 1 cup unsalted butter, softened
- 2 cups granulated sugar
- 4 large eggs
- 1 teaspoon vanilla extract
- 1 cup buttermilk
- 1/2 cup coconut milk
- Zest of 2 limes
- Juice of 2 limes

For the coconut lime curd filling:

- 1 cup granulated sugar
- 4 large eggs
- 1/2 cup fresh lime juice (from about 4-5 limes)
- Zest of 2 limes
- 1/4 cup unsalted butter, cut into small pieces
- 1 cup shredded coconut (sweetened or unsweetened)

For the coconut lime buttercream frosting:

- 1 1/2 cups unsalted butter, softened
- 6 cups powdered sugar
- Zest of 1 lime
- Juice of 1 lime
- 1/2 teaspoon coconut extract
- 2-4 tablespoons coconut milk (as needed for consistency)
- Toasted coconut flakes and lime slices for garnish

Instructions:

1. Make the cake:
    - Preheat your oven to 350°F (175°C). Grease and flour three 8-inch round cake pans.
    - In a medium bowl, whisk together the cake flour, baking powder, baking soda, and salt.
    - In a large bowl, cream together the butter and sugar until light and fluffy.

- Add eggs one at a time, beating well after each addition. Stir in the vanilla extract.
- In another bowl, combine the buttermilk, coconut milk, lime zest, and lime juice.
- Gradually add the dry ingredients to the butter mixture, alternating with the buttermilk mixture, beginning and ending with the dry ingredients. Mix until just combined.
- Divide the batter evenly among the prepared pans and smooth the tops.
- Bake for 25-30 minutes, or until a toothpick inserted into the center comes out clean.
- Allow the cakes to cool in the pans for 10 minutes, then transfer to wire racks to cool completely.

2. Make the coconut lime curd filling:
   - In a medium saucepan, whisk together the sugar, eggs, lime juice, and lime zest.
   - Cook over medium heat, stirring constantly, until the mixture thickens and coats the back of a spoon (about 8-10 minutes).
   - Remove from heat and stir in the butter until melted and well combined.
   - Stir in the shredded coconut. Transfer the curd to a bowl and press a piece of plastic wrap directly onto the surface to prevent a skin from forming.
   - Chill in the refrigerator until firm.

3. Make the coconut lime buttercream frosting:
   - In a large bowl, beat the softened butter until creamy.
   - Gradually add the powdered sugar, one cup at a time, beating well after each addition.
   - Add lime zest, lime juice, and coconut extract. Beat until light and fluffy.
   - Add coconut milk, one tablespoon at a time, until the frosting reaches a smooth and spreadable consistency.

4. Assemble the cake:
   - Place one cake layer on a serving plate or cake stand.
   - Spread a layer of coconut lime curd filling over the cake layer.
   - Repeat with the remaining cake layers and filling.
   - Frost the entire cake with the coconut lime buttercream frosting, smoothing the sides and top.

5. Decorate the cake:
   - Garnish the top of the cake with toasted coconut flakes and slices of lime for a beautiful and tropical look.
   - Optionally, sprinkle more toasted coconut around the base of the cake for added decoration.

6. Chill the cake until ready to serve to allow the flavors to meld together.

This Coconut Lime Wedding Cake will be a delightful and refreshing addition to your special day, combining the tropical flavors of coconut and lime in a beautiful and elegant dessert. Enjoy!

Honey Walnut Wedding Cake

Ingredients:

For the cake:

- 3 cups all-purpose flour
- 1 tablespoon baking powder
- 1/2 teaspoon baking soda
- 1/2 teaspoon salt
- 1 cup unsalted butter, softened
- 1 1/2 cups granulated sugar
- 4 large eggs
- 1 teaspoon vanilla extract
- 1 cup buttermilk
- 1 cup chopped walnuts

For the honey walnut filling:

- 1/2 cup honey
- 1/2 cup unsalted butter
- 1/2 cup chopped walnuts

For the honey cream cheese frosting:

- 1 cup unsalted butter, softened
- 8 oz cream cheese, softened
- 1/4 cup honey
- 4 cups powdered sugar
- 1 teaspoon vanilla extract

Instructions:

1. Make the cake:
    - Preheat your oven to 350°F (175°C). Grease and flour three 8-inch round cake pans.
    - In a medium bowl, whisk together the flour, baking powder, baking soda, and salt.
    - In a large bowl, cream together the butter and sugar until light and fluffy.
    - Add eggs one at a time, beating well after each addition. Stir in the vanilla extract.
    - Gradually add the dry ingredients to the butter mixture, alternating with the buttermilk, beginning and ending with the dry ingredients. Mix until just combined.
    - Fold in the chopped walnuts.
    - Divide the batter evenly among the prepared pans and smooth the tops.
    - Bake for 25-30 minutes, or until a toothpick inserted into the center comes out clean.

- Allow the cakes to cool in the pans for 10 minutes, then transfer to wire racks to cool completely.
2. Make the honey walnut filling:
    - In a small saucepan, melt the butter and honey together over medium heat, stirring constantly.
    - Stir in the chopped walnuts and cook for 1-2 minutes, until the mixture thickens slightly.
    - Remove from heat and let cool completely before using as filling.
3. Make the honey cream cheese frosting:
    - In a large bowl, beat together the softened butter and cream cheese until smooth and creamy.
    - Gradually add the powdered sugar, one cup at a time, beating well after each addition.
    - Stir in the honey and vanilla extract until well combined and the frosting is smooth.
4. Assemble the cake:
    - Place one cake layer on a serving plate or cake stand.
    - Spread a layer of honey walnut filling over the cake layer.
    - Repeat with the remaining cake layers and filling.
    - Frost the entire cake with the honey cream cheese frosting, smoothing the sides and top.
5. Decorate the cake:
    - Optionally, garnish the top of the cake with additional chopped walnuts for texture and decoration.
    - Drizzle a little extra honey over the top for added sweetness and shine.
6. Chill the cake until ready to serve to allow the flavors to meld together.

This Honey Walnut Wedding Cake will be a delightful addition to your celebration, with its rich honey flavor, crunchy walnuts, and creamy frosting creating a perfect balance of textures and tastes. Enjoy this special cake with your loved ones!

Lavender Honey Wedding Cake

Ingredients:

For the lavender honey cake layers:

- 3 cups cake flour
- 1 tablespoon baking powder
- 1/2 teaspoon baking soda
- 1/2 teaspoon salt
- 1 cup unsalted butter, softened
- 1 1/2 cups granulated sugar
- 4 large eggs
- 1 teaspoon vanilla extract
- 1 cup buttermilk
- 1/4 cup honey
- 2 tablespoons culinary lavender buds, finely ground (use food processor or mortar and pestle)

For the lavender honey buttercream frosting:

- 1 1/2 cups unsalted butter, softened
- 6 cups powdered sugar
- 1/4 cup honey
- 1-2 tablespoons culinary lavender buds, finely ground
- 2-4 tablespoons heavy cream or milk (as needed for consistency)

For decoration (optional):

- Fresh lavender sprigs
- Edible flowers

Instructions:

1. Make the lavender honey cake layers:
    - Preheat your oven to 350°F (175°C). Grease and flour three 8-inch round cake pans.
    - In a medium bowl, whisk together the cake flour, baking powder, baking soda, and salt.
    - In a separate bowl, cream together the butter and sugar until light and fluffy.
    - Add eggs one at a time, beating well after each addition. Stir in the vanilla extract.
    - In another bowl, combine the buttermilk, honey, and finely ground lavender buds.
    - Gradually add the dry ingredients to the butter mixture, alternating with the buttermilk mixture, beginning and ending with the dry ingredients. Mix until just combined.

- Divide the batter evenly among the prepared pans and smooth the tops.
- Bake for 25-30 minutes, or until a toothpick inserted into the center comes out clean.
- Allow the cakes to cool in the pans for 10 minutes, then transfer to wire racks to cool completely.
2. Make the lavender honey buttercream frosting:
    - In a large bowl, beat the softened butter until creamy.
    - Gradually add the powdered sugar, one cup at a time, beating well after each addition.
    - Stir in the honey and finely ground lavender buds.
    - Add heavy cream or milk, one tablespoon at a time, until the frosting reaches a smooth and spreadable consistency.
3. Assemble the cake:
    - Place one cake layer on a serving plate or cake stand.
    - Spread a layer of lavender honey buttercream frosting over the cake layer.
    - Repeat with the remaining cake layers and frosting.
    - Frost the entire cake with the remaining lavender honey buttercream frosting, smoothing the sides and top.
4. Decorate the cake:
    - Optionally, garnish the top of the cake with fresh lavender sprigs and edible flowers for a beautiful and fragrant presentation.
5. Chill the cake until ready to serve to allow the flavors to meld together.

This Lavender Honey Wedding Cake will be a stunning addition to your special day, with its delicate lavender flavor complemented by the sweetness of honey in a moist and tender cake. Enjoy this elegant dessert with your guests!